Teen Time

Working out What You Want & Choosing How to 'Be'

(A guide for navigating the teenage years)

Helen Middleton

First published by Busybird Publishing 2018
Copyright © 2018 Helen Middleton

ISBN
Print: 978-1-925830-01-9

Helen Middleton has asserted her right under the Copyright, Designs and Patents Act 1988 to be identified as the author of this work. The information in this book is based on the author's experiences and opinions. The publisher specifically disclaims responsibility for any adverse consequences, which may result from use of the information contained herein. Permission to use information has been sought by the author. Any breaches will be rectified in further editions of the book.

All rights reserved. No part of this publication may be reproduced, stored in or introduced into a retrieval system, or transmitted in any form, or by any means (electronic, mechanical, photocopying, recording or otherwise) without the prior written permission of the author. Any person who does any unauthorised act in relation to this publication may be liable to criminal prosecution and civil claims for damages. Enquiries should be made through the publisher.

Cover Illustration: Leonie De Salis
Cover Design: Kev Howlett, Busybird Publishing
Layout and typesetting: Busybird Publishing
Editor: Laura McCluskey

Busybird Publishing
2/118 Para Road
Montmorency, Victoria
Australia 3094
www.busybird.com.au

*For my grandchildren – Toby, Lachlan, Matthew, Henry, Emma.
Also, Declan, Thomas, Jessica, and James.
My great nieces and nephews.*

Contents

Acknowledgements	i
Preface	iii
Introduction	v
1. Upfront with school issues	**3**
1.1. When it all seems too hard	3
1.2. Dealing with bullies	12
1.3. Does your teacher have it in for you?	27
1.4. Have you been acting dumb to avoid getting stirred?	28
1.5. How to avoid feeling overwhelmed in Senior School	29
1.6. The last year of school: an emotional time	31
2. Friends	**35**
2.1. When friendship groups chop and change	37
2.2. Friendships that hurt	38
2.3. Being liked vs. being popular	40
2.4. Making close, intimate friendships	41
2.5. Becoming more assertive	44
2.6. The lure of drugs	47
2.7. Social media and gaming	50
2.8. When friends are in trouble	54
2.9. Dating	57
3. Starting work	**59**
3.1. Your first job interview	61
3.2. What does it mean to be treated with dignity?	64
3.3. How to deal with a difficult boss	66
3.4. Bullying in the workplace	68

3.5.	Knowing your rights	69
3.6.	Having fun at work	70

4. Family issues 73

4.1.	Seeking increased freedom	75
4.2.	When your friends feel unsafe	78
4.3.	Making your stepfamily work	79
4.4.	Coping with siblings	81
4.5.	Game playing	84
4.6.	Negativity and attitude	87

5. Emotions 91

5.1.	Building and valuing your self-esteem	93
5.2.	Resilience: growing and learning from mistakes	96
5.3.	Overcoming loneliness	98
5.4.	Sexuality	102
5.5.	Falling in love	114
5.6.	Understanding grief	115
5.7.	When everything seems hopeless	118
5.8.	Overcoming stress, overthinking, and anxiety	121
5.9.	Self-harming behaviours	132
5.10.	Controlling your anger	134
5.11.	Resilience and leadership	137

6. Taking risks 139

6.1.	Physical and emotional risks	141
6.2.	Which is worse – taking, or not taking risks?	142
6.3.	Finding your edge	144
6.4.	Attracting good luck	146
6.5.	Feeling real	148
6.6.	Changing the scripts in your head	149
6.7.	Good and bad decisions	153
6.8.	Your future	155

7. Nurturing your soul 159

7.1.	Believing in yourself	161
7.2.	Spirituality and you	163
7.3.	Going forward	168

About the author 171

Acknowledgements

I would like to acknowledge my many colleagues over the years. These include teachers, guidance officers, principals, deputy principals, gestalt and family therapists, psychotherapists, psychologists, youth workers, social workers, nurses, general practitioners, and other mental health professionals. I thank those who educated and trained me, and I especially thank all the psychotherapy theorists and practitioners whose ideas I have tried to weave into practical applications in this book. I am grateful to those friends and colleagues who have helped in the process of editing. I would particularly like to thank Leonie de Salis for her rich and creative illustrations.

Lastly, I would like to thank the many clients who honoured me by openly sharing their world with me. So often I have admired their fortitude, wisdom, and humour.

Preface

My enjoyment of adolescents has spanned more than 45 years. I was always involved in various youth leadership programs, then became a teacher working in Melbourne, Hobart, Adelaide, and Brisbane. I trained and worked as a secondary school guidance officer in Brisbane from 1991-2006, then moved to Hobart in 2006 where I continued to work with young people at Headspace (2009-2018), as well as in private practice.

I never cease to be amazed by the resourcefulness of young people. My mind flashes over the young people I have worked with; those who have survived being shunted from foster home to foster home, and those who have been physically, sexually, and/or emotionally abused. I think of those who have preferred to live on the street or to couch-surf rather than be with their family, and those who have been carers for ill, suicidal, or self-harming parents.

When young people know they are not under threat they willingly open up to tell their story. They are often keen to talk with an adult who is not their parent. Talking with a school counsellor or other trusted adult is a great opportunity to practice adult conversation. While their issues often seem superficial at first, sooner or later the deeper story emerges.

I learned early on that once you take the time to listen and stay with a young person's story, it becomes easy to understand how they see the world the way they do, why their choices may have been poor, and why they feel overwhelmed by their situation. Their sense of loneliness often comes from thinking that others around them do not have similar difficulties. Over the years I have been honoured to witness so many journeys – some painful, some horrific, and some joyous. I feel privileged to have been emotionally connected to young people, even if only for a moment, as they shared their most intimate struggles, and I appreciate their unique survival skills. I have enjoyed finding ways to validate them, as well as challenge them with new perspectives of their situation.

I am sad that, while I have been able to help other peoples' children, I will not be around to help the future generations of children in my own family. My challenge in this book is to capture the wisdom connected to issues that commonly trouble young people, and to record it in a way that is easy for them to quickly flip to anything that might hold their interest. It is very likely that many will have absolutely no interest in reading something written by an older person, and it is quite possible that what I write today will be totally out of date within 10 years. However, I have a hunch that while new problems emerge, the underlying thought patterns change very little.

I take the risk of writing this anyway, because I care that my grandchildren and their children are given every assistance possible. I want them to make wise choices that generate confidence, independence, and the resilience to be able to handle any opportunities and challenges that come their way. Life will always be full of ups and downs which, when taken in one's stride, become merely bumps in the road.

I hesitate and question the danger in providing too many answers instead of allowing young people to find wonder and meaning in their own life journey. At the same time, having been witness to the complex struggles typically confronting young people, I am hopeful that an enriched knowledge base will enhance personal growth and kick-start a journey with infinite possibilities. My purpose in writing this book will be well served if only one element of this book provides a stitch-in-time for one young reader.

Introduction

The following chapters are structured to highlight common issues presented to me by young people during counselling sessions. It has a 'pick and choose' style, rather than being a 'read all' kind of book. Some topics will hold more interest than others.

Trusting the resourcefulness of young people, I have avoided information that might be sourced easily using future technology. I have avoided step-by-step strategies, and have tried to introduce bigger picture thoughts and perspectives that might encourage wise choice-making.

There are various themes running through the book: self-responsibility, controlled risk-taking, trusting your own emotions, overcoming fear, shame, and anxious thinking, as well as maintaining life balance through good decision-making. The ultimate purpose of these themes is to bring some wisdom to any life circumstance in which you find yourself.

Wisdom helps you to live with, rather than fear complexity. Anxious thoughts that are paralysing can also harness you into action. Simplicity in life can be created by choosing to live in the here and now; tempered, of course, by good sense and future planning. The skill of knowing what you want is something that requires practice. The book encourages you to grow in your ability to **work out what you want** and **choose how you want to be**.

The power of want will forge through any anxious thought. In any situation you can choose wisely how you deal with your world. This will help protect you against those who set out to hurt, and give you the capacity to follow any pathway you choose.

Nurture and believe in yourself. Love unconditionally, but not stupidly. Work hard to be the best you can be for the sake of those who love you. Greet lies with honesty, turn tears into smiles, and hardship into challenge. Trust in your own wisdom. It will lift you to another level of emotion, thought, and morality.

It is my hope that these writings will help to weave wisdom through your thoughts as you flip through the pages. Whether you are a young person, parent, or someone who works with young people, I hope it will assist you in finding the appropriate words to talk about the issues. If you have the words to talk about how you feel and what you think, the experience of talking to someone else about your deeply-felt emotions is life changing. It will move you to a much less troubling place and bring you new perspectives for the future.

Helen Middleton

5 July 2018

Chapter 1

1

Upfront with school issues

1.1. When it all seems too hard

1.2. Dealing with bullies

1.3. Does your teacher have it in for you?

1.4. Have you been acting dumb to avoid getting stirred?

1.5. How to avoid feeling overwhelmed in Senior School

1.6. The last year of school: an emotional time

1.1. When it all seems too hard

Challenges in the Middle School years

'I can't concentrate,' is one of the most common complaints amongst Middle School students. It can be hard to keep your attention on something you have no interest in. It can also be really hard if you are not in tune with your teacher. Even if you are bored with a particular topic or subject, try to treat it as just one task that has to be done. Find just one thing that is new for you.

School can be challenging in all sorts of ways. Maybe you have changed schools, or started a new class, or you've got a new teacher who has a different teaching style. Once you work out what the real issue is, you can start to find creative ways to fix the problem.

If it is hard to understand your teacher, it does not necessarily mean that you are the problem. Teachers teach in many different ways. What works for you may not work for other students, and vice versa. Some learners like the big picture first and detail later, or the other way around. Others prefer ideas to be presented visually, like having pie charts, graphs, or pictures. Then there are those who prefer reading written material, or listening to someone talk about the topic.

It helps if you know what you prefer; is it easier to remember something you have seen, heard, or read? Are you more of an experiential learner, or a kinaesthetic learner? An experiential learner likes doing and being involved in some kind of experience. Kinaesthetic learners like to move about while they are learning. Maybe you are happy with all kinds of learning. Think about it: when you are flying on a task and really getting it, what are you doing? Treat it as a challenge to learn from material presented in different ways. If you really have to master something, convert the task to the mode of learning you prefer, e.g. you prefer to dance around while you are learning a verse of poetry. That is okay, as long as it works for you.

If a lack of concentration is causing your problems, think about what is going on. Are you too tired because of late nights or being over-committed with sport or other activities? Are you too distracted because of dramas on social media? All adults have been there. Reflect on this, and be brave enough to make some changes. Maybe there are lots of things that are not major, even better – make some little changes.

When you feel overwhelmed and unable to make things better it is possibly due to a number of stresses. Put together, they seem big. On their own, they are probably easy to fix. It helps to make a diagram of all the stressors, and then work to make some changes in each of the areas. Try something like this:

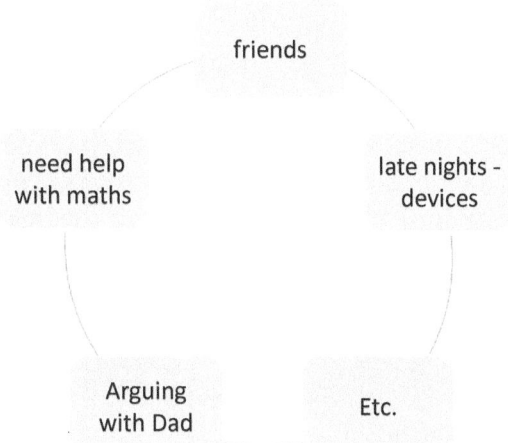

Add in as many text boxes as you like. Write down your distractions, one in each circle. These might be any of the following (or maybe you have some unique ones of your own):

Personal Distractions	**School Distractions**
• Can't say no to friends • Distracted by 'love' issues • Life feels unfulfilling • Worried about home/parents • Can't get started • Feeling depressed • Feeling lazy and unmotivated • Junk food • No breakfast • Computer games • Over committed • Feeling anxious • Too much partying • Fighting with Mum, Dad or siblings	• Hate my subjects • Need help with Maths • Teacher doesn't like me • Friend dramas • Being bullied • No idea which career to pick • No quiet place to work • Social media • Crummy group of friends • Trying too hard to be cool

If you found the above exercise difficult, try keeping a journal every day for a week. Write down all the things you did not like about your day, or the things that distracted you. At the end of the week, try the exercise again.

Sometimes there are really tough things to deal with in life. Is there something you find really hard to talk about? Do you make your own stress by trying so hard to be perfect? Do you try too hard to make everyone like you? Do you feel anxious about getting into trouble? Do you feel too scared to put up your hand to contribute to class discussion? Are you always feeding yourself negative messages? Once you can identify the issues making you unhappy, you have taken the first step towards feeling better.

The next step is to take the initiative to do something to diminish the reasons you are unhappy. If the out of school issues are too pressing, look for opportunities to talk to a responsible adult about them. Sometimes life hurts. When life has gone wrong, it can take a while to heal the hurt. Find someone you can trust to keep your discussion confidential.

Some solutions will become clear to you the minute you acknowledge the real problem. Most problems can be viewed from different perspectives. Sometimes it is valuable to talk to someone about the things you find hard because problems are often created in our own heads. When you make even one small change in the right direction, there will be a ripple effect where other aspects of life all start to change, as well.

You will be successful at study if you are well-organised and are prepared to have a go. You will learn from the experience, even if you get it wrong. Of course, you have to persist and follow through with your effort. Giving up is easy to do, but hanging in there is what brings you rewards. The harder the task is, the more you have to keep trying, and the greater the reward will be.

It is smart to call for support and help. If you accept that you are having difficulty with something then it is easy to get help.

Be kind to yourself and take a risk. Don't be afraid to fail. Coach yourself, saying, 'If I mess up this time, I'll get it right next time.'

Remember, if you set goals, plan your time, try hard, and ask for help when you need it, you will be successful with your schoolwork. If you are kind to and tolerant of others, and you play by the rules, you will have good friends.

- So what exactly is it that causes you stress?
- Challenge yourself to make small positive changes.
- Start to do something about it.

Leave your worries at the school gate

It is easy to be distracted by family and life events outside of school. If this is a big issue for you, try to adopt the policy that the minute you walk through the school gate you leave your worries outside. They will be back there when you leave school at the end of the day, so it is okay to park them.

Learning to focus when you least feel like it is a real skill. Try really hard to focus in the first few minutes of each lesson when the teacher explains what the lesson will be about. This will help the whole flow of the lesson. Put effort into working out what the teacher is trying to impart to you, whether or not they have good teaching skills. Look at your eating habits – you may need energy food.

When your energy levels are high, make sure you put in maximum effort rather than be socialising. Avoid falling into the trap of talking when you are supposed to be working quietly. It is a little foolish if you find yourself socialising in class and doing classwork in your lunch breaks. Have fun in your breaks and work hard in class.

- Do the right thing at the right time.
- Leave home problems behind at the school gate.
- Really focus in the first few minutes of each lesson.
- Enjoy your day.

Make homework work for you

Homework doesn't have to be a nightmare. Yes, it sometimes seems pointless. Homework is not just about getting extra work done. When you enter the senior years or go to tertiary study, you will find it really hard to cope if you are not in the habit of being able to sit down at home and study independently. It is like training for a sporting final. You have to do the training before you front for the Grand Final.

Be prepared to put in time with homework and study on a regular basis. With set homework, be clear about what is required before you leave school. Choose to start on the hardest task first. When you have knocked that over, the rest will seem easy. If you leave it 'til last, it will be like a heavy cloud hanging over you, and may encourage you to procrastinate, or do nothing. If you are a chronic procrastinator, make it your goal to start a little homework at the designated time. Just make yourself do one small part of your homework and celebrate your success in achieving that. Success with one bit will lead to another. Before you know it, you will have built up your homework time every night.

Have a clear space at home to do your study. Put your devices in another room. Turn off any social media alerts on your computer. Seek your parent or caregiver's assistance in stopping any interruptions from friends or family. Turn off music. No matter how much you convince yourself that music helps, many investigations have shown it to be a distraction. Don't kid yourself that hearing your favourite song won't distract you. Music is highly emotive and, while it is wonderful for you, it is better to finish your work efficiently and have time to chill out and fully listen to your music. Turn off your other social media devices – those little flashing signs alerting you to messages will be a distraction. Use it as a treat, something you can check once your study task is completed. Use self-discipline. You will be well-rewarded.

Learn to say no to distractions. Focus 100% on your work. If you focus and work efficiently, you may find it fully-engaging. You might actually enjoy it! Even if you don't, then having 100% attention will ensure the tasks are done and out of the way, leaving you free to enjoy your favourite activities as your reward. Think of it this way; everyone has the same amount of time in class. If you want to do particularly well, then a little extra study and effort outside school is what will help you achieve the results you want.

- Music is highly emotive. It will distract you while you study.
- Move your social media devices to another room.
- Learn to say no to distractions. Focus 100% on your work.

Try being super organised
There are a few tricks to being organised. Make yourself a study calendar. Firstly, mark down all the activities you really love, like sports training, music rehearsals, or work shifts. Write down one or two TV programs you cannot bear to miss. Then, add family and social engagements. Mark down some chill-out time, e.g. a Sunday sleep-in.

For assignment tasks where you have weeks to prepare, mark down the due dates in red. Also write down test dates in red. Mark the day you need to start preparing your assignments in green, as well as the days you need to start studying for your tests. Stand back. Take stock of the busy weeks. Look at the big picture and observe how little time you have in which to be super organised.

Once you have your date calendar organised, draw up a weekly planner for your set homework and study. Black out some time each night for your homework according to the general work flow you experience. If you have double English on Tuesday, then you can be pretty sure you will have English homework on Tuesday evening. Make sure there is a time for each subject.

Once this is done, add in your study time each day. This is time to do personal study, like reading over material again, drawing up lists of vocabulary or formulae that you have to rote learn. It is time to summarise textbooks in readiness for future tests. Then you will need time for assignments. Maybe you need a block of time to really get into an assignment. Perhaps you need to dedicate two hours on a Sunday afternoon to do assignments.

Above all, build in some reward time. If you complete your homework and study tasks during the week, treat yourself with special time off, perhaps Friday evening – time to see friends, or chill at home, whatever you choose. If you get to Friday night and you have been slack, then it is a no-go. This becomes your catch-up time, and you have missed your reward.

Remember, your planner is a guide only, and it needs to be regarded as flowing and flexible. Students often throw study calendars out because they can't stick to them. Sometimes there will be distractions. Life will get in the way. For instance, if your parent or caregiver says on Thursday evening, 'Come on, we need to go buy those new sport shoes', then you need to be flexible. At the same time, you need to calculate when you will be able to make up the study hours you are losing by going out.

The weekly planner becomes a flowing, yet flexible plan. The basics have to be achieved sometime, if not necessarily at the time listed on the planner. Create a realistic weekly planner that is not too harsh. Be strict with makeup time, even if it means getting up at 6am to fit the work into your busy day.

- The key to academic success is to be well-organised.
- Sort your resources quickly and start tasks early.
- Put the finished task aside for a day.
- Review and refine before you hand it in.

Limit your stress

Everyone needs stress. It gives you the energy to get going. Stress is a normal part of living – it is what motivates you to do the things you need to do. Stress encourages you to meet deadlines and follow through with tasks. This is stress in the healthy zone.

When lots of things happen at once, or you worry too much, then your stress can take you out of your healthy zone. Monitor your own stress levels. If you are feeling uncomfortably stressed, then work out what it is that is driving your stress.

Are you

- trying too hard to be perfect?
- leaving things to the last moment?
- allowing your schedule to be way too busy?
- setting unrealistic expectations for yourself?
- letting your brain control you, instead of you controlling of it?

Take stock of what is going on in the cognitive part of your brain, i.e. the thinking part. Try to become skilled at giving your brain a positive direction, instead of forever being at the mercy of negative patterns of thinking. Tell your brain what you want it to become engaged with, and exactly what you want it to focus on. Take charge of it like you do a computer or an interactive computer game. Use it as a tool, instead of getting lost in it.

> - What are your stress drivers? Assess them ... are they helpful, or do they diminish your effort?
> - Use your brain like you do a computer.
> - Call on it when you need its help to problem-solve.

1.2. Dealing with bullies

The hurtful nature of bullying

Around the age of 13-14 years, girls are renowned for behaving in nasty ways. It happens in all schools. It may be open and direct, or sophisticated and behind-the-scenes. Girls form into groups and often torment others in subtle ways that teachers don't see. Girls of this age will often boast that they have a large group good friends. They interpret this as popularity, and think it will continue forever. Time shows that it is really hard to sustain a large group of friends without conflict emerging at some point.

In bolstering their own sense of importance, these girls can gang up and exclude other members of the group, then change their mind the next day. It can very much be a 'We are best friends today, but tomorrow we are not.' This controlling behaviour serves to bolster the initiator's own sense of importance. In this age group, most girls are insecure about themselves in every way. Some try to mask this insecurity by acting bold and powerful in an attempt to bolster their own self-esteem.

Some girls relish opportunities to spread rumours. Some can be masters at subtle exclusion and backstabbing. They are often led by one or two who wield power. The behaviour can be very nasty and cruel, and is often targeted at girls who are either too nice or vulnerable to fight back. When enough is enough, battlelines are drawn, and the social culture can quickly become quite toxic for all involved. Whole classes of girls can get caught into this nastiness, with the result that they all start to feel insecure, unwanted, unloved, and miserable.

If you are wise you will choose not to be involved in any of this and will see it for what it is, unsociable and inappropriate. It is important to focus on your own life and the good things that make you happy, rather than the constant drama that surrounds nasty behaviour. It is often fuelled by social media, and never ends well.

If you are targeted with cyberbullying, take a screenshot of the messages on your phone or computer, and show them to someone who you trust. Keep a record and build your case, ready to report. Be careful not to lower yourself to nasty retaliation. Stay out of it, and report it. Pick the most helpful teacher and ask for the incident to be recorded. Once it is reported and written down by the teacher, it becomes part of your ongoing evidence about an illegal activity.

On the sidelines are often those calm and sensible young women who allow themselves to suffer from self-esteem issues because they are excluded from the 'cool' group. If you are one of these, be patient; you will soon see this nasty group break itself up through constant friction that inevitably reaches a crisis. These groups often self-destruct as each member of the group becomes unhappy.

Be very wary if you are caught up in this kind of nastiness. Step back and evaluate. If you are being cruel, stop. If you are the target, let someone know what you are dealing with. Remember, behind-the-scenes nastiness can be just as hurtful as a physical threat, and it is not something you want to join, put up with, or stay silent about.

Boys are usually less devious and or subtle in their bullying. They are often more physical, more direct, and more open with their threats and aggression. Their bullying can be just as emotionally brutal, and should never be tolerated. If you are the target of this kind of bullying, note that it always happens outside of adult supervision which indicates that the perpetrators know full well that they are doing the wrong thing. No matter what they have said to you, you are not the problem. Anyone who bullies does so through a need to feel strong and powerful because underneath they are quite insecure and vulnerable.

Intimidation can be subtle; taking your lunch, or dobbing you in to a teacher when you have done nothing. This kind of behaviour can be really distressing, and while it might be laughed off at first, if it is ongoing it needs to be stopped.

Typically, the more severe bullying behaviour includes things like, 'If you tell anyone I'll beat you up' or, 'Give me your lunch money and don't tell anyone or I will bash up your brother'. This kind of direct intimidation needs to be reported straight away.

It is really important to remember that threats and verbal humiliation are very daunting for anyone on the receiving end of them, regardless of age or stage of life. You do NOT have to put up with bullying behaviour of any kind.

Self-check: do you contribute to the problem in any way?

It is important to ask yourself if there is anything you are doing to incite a bully's behaviour. For instance, have you called this person names, made nasty gestures, or told any lies about them? Have you showed, through your body language, that you don't like them? Have you snubbed them, or just generally found a way to get under their skin?

It is important to be really honest with yourself, because if you don't change your behaviour it is going to make it very hard to change your situation. If you truly want to make things better, then you need to be squeaky-clean in all your dealings from now on. Be clear on what you want, i.e. for the bullying to stop. If you just want to win and be the bigger bully, then this problem won't get solved. A real win is when you get to relax without the feeling that they will get you back at any time.

It may be that you are a bystander. If you see bullying behaviour and do nothing, then you are, in effect, condoning the bullying behaviour. Of course, this needs to be tempered with good sense. As a bystander, it may be dangerous to step into severe bullying, but you can take immediate action and let someone know. This could mean calling the police, or finding a staff member. At the very least you can report what you saw or heard. You can also support the target of the bullying by reassuring them that the behaviour you witnessed is unacceptable and that it is not their fault. Be kind and encouraging.

If there is no behaviour you personally need to fix up, then it will be useful to work out the way that the bully is niggling you. Is this person getting to you over something you are sensitive about? Bullies can be quite skilful at latching onto things people really care about. They work hard at being powerful – they watch and learn from your reactions to identify a weak spot.

A weak spot is something you feel super sensitive about. This is a good opportunity to really look at yourself squarely. So what if you have big ears, are shorter or taller, or bigger or skinnier than others? So what if your family is rich or poor, and if you don't like the same music? Every aspect of you is unique. What will make you a great person is a measure of how much you will contribute to this world and the fact that you don't need to bully someone else.

As long as you are not the one who is doing the bullying then you can be comforted knowing that you are the mature, sensible person. You're someone who does not need to go around being nasty and horrible in order to make yourself feel good. Bullies bully because they are incredibly insecure and immature. You are okay!

Bullies are found at all ages and in all walks of life. You will always come across people determined to find someone on whom they can unleash their venom. These kinds of people need to throw their weight around because it is the only way they feel powerful. If it is not your frizzy hair, the way you walk, the shape of your nose, the way you talk, or the way your ears stick out, then one thing is certain – these bullies will find something else. What bullies pick on is irrelevant, so don't take it personally. If you are unaffected they will move on to someone else. If they get you upset, they are likely to keep going because they think they have found an easy target. Shrug them off.

Very often bullies target those who are bright and successful. This is known as tall poppy syndrome. It is the idea that you have to cut someone down to size if they impress or stand out from the crowd. It is a sad quirk in Australian culture.

If a bully gets no reaction from you, they will move on to another person. Here is where you hold the power. Show the bully a poker face so he or she does not see that the arrow has gone straight into your heart. Try to appear dreadfully bored with the whole thing. If you are able to show, by your body language or words, that their comments don't bother you, then you will defuel the bully.

Look the bully in the eye and say, 'Oh, grow up!' or, 'Get a life.' Crack a joke and say something like, 'Gee, that's a weak one today,' or even just, 'Boring!' Humour helps in any situation. Let the bully see that you are not prepared to waste emotional energy on someone you don't like or respect. Support yourself emotionally. Internally, ask yourself, 'Do I go around bullying other people?' Hopefully not!

No one likes or respects a bully. Whatever comes out of their mouth is not worth taking any notice of. You don't like or respect people who behave like this, so why care about anything they say? It is not worth wasting emotional energy on them.

- Let the bully see that you are not prepared to waste emotional energy on them.
- Remember, the bully is not someone you like or respect, so what they say is irrelevant.
- Save your emotional energy for people you like and respect.

What to do if bullying persists or becomes physical

Assuming you do not go around bullying others in order to feel good about yourself, then you are NOT the problem. The person who bullies has an unhealthy need to be bigger or better than other people by standing over them, excluding them, or trying to make them feel small in some way. These are the only strategies the bullies have to make themselves feel big. Don't make the bullying your problem by believing anything they say.

Bullies know they are doing the wrong thing. This is why they don't choose to bully in front of an adult in authority. They choose a time when others are not around. Sometimes even the threat of reporting will curb their behaviour. You can say, 'Give it a break ... do that one more time and I will have to report you!'

Like yourself and be happy with who you are. When you do this, you will have no need to go around making other people's lives miserable just so you can feel powerful. Be proud of who you are and what other good people think of you. When you stand up to a bully, the bully will slink away. They may spit nasty words at you as they go, but you will know you have put them in their place. Remember, we meet bullies all through life. This is a good time to learn how to deal with them. It is also a good opportunity to get strong and solid in yourself.

Say over and over to yourself, 'I am ok. The bully is the one with the insecurity problem.' Who cares what they think or say?

Don't be lowered to their pathetic behaviour. Say, 'I am not going to waste any emotional energy on a bully.' Be consistent in your bored attitude towards them and be persistent in your self-talk. Never give in.

> Why do bullies act so tough?
> I think they must have had life rough,
> Why else do they make others small?
> If not to make themselves feel tall.
>
> But I know this pathetic game
> And I'm proud of the way others know my name
> There's no way I'll be made a fool
> So I'll walk away and know I AM COOL!

If bullying is getting beyond your ability to handle it with a little humour, tell someone. If you are being physically hurt or attacked then you must immediately report it to your parents, and/or teachers. Everyone has a right to feel safe. When you report, you are choosing to stand up for yourself and your rights. You are also standing up for the rights of other students. In particular, you are asserting the rights of all students to feel safe.

Remember:
- The bully is the one with the problem.
- No-one respects a bully!
- When you stand up to a bully, he or she will slink away.
- A bully will only get away with it if you don't report them.

When enough is enough
If there is an ongoing pattern of bullying, rather than a one-off event, it is time to think smart. Teachers cannot be all-seeing or all-hearing. It is no use talking about what the bully said or did 10 days ago. Write everything down as it happens. Record the full picture of when, where, how often, and what they said or did. If you can produce a day-by-day record of persistent bullying, then staff members have detailed data with which to nail the offending student. Remember that the law, teachers, and professionals are on your side. Bullying should never be tolerated. Keeping a record gives teachers what they need to take action.

Sometimes bullying is so minor that it seems silly to complain. There is an unwritten code that you should just ignore it, and not make a fuss as a first line strategy. Another student might give you a one-off death stare, or 'accidentally' bump into you, or knock your pens off your desk. It can be really irritating. Unfortunately, complaining about these things can sound like you are being a little precious, and you may feel like you're wasting your teacher's time. If it is truly a one-off occasion, you probably have the skills to roll your eyes and say, 'Grow up', or to crack a joke. It is always clever to use humour, rather than create conflict by getting angry.

When this sort of bullying occurs a couple of times, it might still be easy to deal with it and dismiss it as stupid. However, when subtle bullying occurs multiple times in a day, it should NOT be ignored. Being deliberately annoyed 5-10 times a day would be enough to make anyone feel harassed, and it is not okay. No adult would, should, or could put up with this kind of harassment – neither should you. If this is happening to you, it is important that you take action.

Say to yourself, 'Right, I'm going to fix this. I'm going to make this stop.' In private, make a record each time something happens. When it does, smile inside yourself and think, *Gotcha!* Discretely make a little note somewhere and then fill out your harassment record when you have some privacy. Keep filling out your record over the next week. Take it to your teacher or year coordinator at the end of the week. The quantity of the harassment will speak for itself.

What will happen next? The teacher is likely to call the culprit aside and give them a severe warning. Remember, the bullying behaviour may not cease just because you have reported it. How does the teacher know if the offending student has continued to bully? Just because it happens again doesn't mean that the teacher didn't do anything.

At this point it is critical that you do not give up and that you keep reporting the bullying behaviour until it stops. Keep another harassment record for the following week. If you don't have any entries on it, then that is great! It will tell you that the situation has changed, and you can start to relax a little. Make sure you start up that record again any time if the bullying occurs again.

Just a reminder: it is important to be squeaky-clean all through this process. That means no egging on or goading, and no provocative body language. You have to be honest. Keep reporting the behaviour. If the bullying continues after you have made a report, you MUST go back and report it again. If you don't do this, teachers will assume that the bullying has stopped. If they don't know, they can't do anything. Take your record back to your teacher and say, 'I am sorry, but it is still going on, even after you warned them. Here is my log.' Each time you do this, the gravity of their behaviour is more obvious and the situation may be escalated to a more senior teacher.

Once identified by teachers, bullies know that if they step over the line again the consequences will be more severe. If you are greeted with the threat, 'If you report me I'll get you after school' or something to that effect, REPORT that, too! Engage your parents' help to ensure your safety. Know that you are doing the right thing.

Record of Bullying/Harassment Behaviours

Day, Date, Time	Where?	What happened?	Name of the bully	Who saw/ heard what happened?	Reported to:

Tips for using this record:

- Make sure you write up this log in private.
- Write everything down, no matter how seemingly insignificant or silly.
- Keep copies – one for you, one for your parents, and one for the teacher.
- Report any physical intimidation immediately.

Many times I have heard parents complain that the school did not handle a bullying incident well. Parents need to remember that administrators handle a huge number of conflicts between students. Mostly they do a fantastic job in resolving conflicts and behavioural issues that you never hear about. Schools are truly amazing institutions. They manage to supervise, organise, and motivate hundreds of students every day. We do this nowhere else in society.

It is difficult for parents. On the one hand, they need to stand up for the rights of their young person, and on the other hand need to understand that situations are often not black and white. Sometimes parents are only prepared to see one side of the situation and feel that their child is being victimised, that the staff do not 'get it'. At the same time, I am sure parents understand that when dealing with squabbling siblings it is often not possible to sort out who started what. Parents need to work with the school staff rather than work against them. The worst thing parents can do is to foster a victim-like attitude while supporting their child to over dramatise what really happened. The table above allows for the honest recording of data that provides evidence.

Some kids will report that they have always been bullied. It becomes like a lifelong story that develops, one that is grounded more in feeling than in fact. If the parent joins in to perpetuate this story and becomes abusive to the staff, the child is disempowered further. It is far more productive to present hard data and have a conversation around how these behaviours might be addressed by the staff. With open and creative discussion with parents, there are many things that can be done at the school level, involving direct intervention with the offending student/s, as well as strategies such as shifting classes or changing environments, buddy systems, supervision areas, community justice restoration processes, etc. This is what needs to be the focus of discussion with school staff.

Too often students won't talk to their parents for fear of them overreacting or getting overly angry and aggressive towards teachers. They think that they can deal with it on their own. They choose to retaliate by getting the bully back in some way. They go one harder to prove they are tougher than their bully. This never works. It only engages the bully even more because it gives them fuel to continue with their behaviours. 'Tit for tat' behaviour only ever escalates. It gets worse and worse until some crime is committed and the police step in.

When parents take things into their own hands they disempower rather than support their young person. The young person needs to be involved in every aspect of the discussion and be encouraged to speak for themselves with the parents' support.

When there is severe bullying, there are two inevitable aspects that need to be attended to. Firstly, the bullying behaviour has to be stopped, and secondly, the target of the bullying needs validation of their rights and assistance in building personal resilience. Records need to be kept even when the bullying has stopped in order to help the target of the bullying realise that it is no longer continuing, that there is no evidence for their story that they have been bullied all their life.

Be confident about your right not to be bullied. You have a right to report any wrongdoing against you and hopefully your school has a no tolerance policy.

- NO-ONE has the right to initimidate you.
- Never give up. Report and report again until the bullying stops.
- Getting back at a bully only engages them more!
- A bully attemps to create fear but they never command respect.
- It is good sense to enlist adult support if you are in any physical danger.

When bullies seem too big and scary

When deciding how to deal with a bully, it is important to assess the risks involved in having anything to do with this individual. Firstly, ask yourself if it is just a feeling you are getting about this person, or has this bully actually threatened or teased you to your face? If your instincts are to stay away from the bully, then listen to them.

Secondly, ask yourself if the bully is a lot bigger or stronger than you. Is there a group, rather than just one? Do you know if the bully is street-smart, or is a known offender? If yes to any of these questions, it is important that you enlist help. With some hardened bullies, it is essential to put as much distance between you two as you can. This is a time when you must involve adults. It is too dangerous not to do so. Unfortunately, the world is not only made up of lovely families. I have known communities where even the police have told me that they cringe when they have to deal with certain families in the area.

You are not soft if you seek support from parents or teachers. It is a mature and sensible course of action if you are being intimidated. If there are threats of physical assault involved, or cruel cyberbullying then it is imperative that you agree to your parents/caregivers involving the police on your behalf.

Make it a point to tell your parents that you want to be involved in everything they do or say to anyone else. Ask them to help you rather than take it out of your hands. It is important that you work collaboratively with them. While it might be good to put distance between you and the bully, if this translates into missing school then this is not on. If you feel you can't face school, then this is a clear sign that both the school and your parents/caregivers need to be involved.

If you feel that you are in any kind of danger, seek help from your parents and the school to ensure your safety. Arrange to walk home with a group of students, or even better, be picked up and delivered to school. Have others with you at all times. It is one thing to shrug off annoying low-level bullying, but another thing to be the target of a physically dangerous bully. They do exist, and bashings do happen, so don't be too determined to sort this yourself. If you can't trust your parents to be cool-headed about the situation, tell a teacher or another trusted adult.

Always remember ...
In time, bullies will move on to someone else – they will get distracted by some other kind of drama creation if their vindictiveness is not refuelled. If you respond, you give them fuel. If you respond with the same kind of mean or nasty behaviour as the bully, this only invites them to escalate the level of their bullying behaviour. This is not what you want. You want distance.

In assessing the situation, you may conclude that your bully is not a hard-nosed offender, just an adolescent throwing their weight around to see how powerful it makes them feel. It might be harder to identify the behaviour of female bullies. They can be skilled in emotional blackmail, emotional isolation, and other demeaning behaviours. They usually target girls who are emotionally vulnerable and their behaviour often goes under the radar.

Intimidation is when someone towers over you or becomes so aggressive that you feel you can't move in any direction. It is the moving so close to you that invades your space, making you feel uncomfortable. There may be the raising of an arm or clenching a fist, a real or pretend strike, or verbal abuse. It usually gets worse unless it is stopped.

A bully knows they are doing the wrong thing. If their sense of power tells them that they can get away with it, they will continue. Bullies relish the opportunity to show their mates the extent of their power.

Remember, you can never be small if you respect yourself and take pride in the way you behave towards others. You have a right to feel safe. No one has a right to intimidate you. If you choose not to report then you are playing into the bully's hands. This is exactly what they want – to keep you quiet and to keep bullying you. Don't get sucked in by this sort of tactic. Parents, teachers, and the law are on your side. They have many ways of dealing with these issues and will always want to look after your safety.

- You can never be 'small' if you respect yourself and take pride in the way you behave toward others.
- Don't get sucked into bullying tactics. There is always a way to make them stop.

Resisting the temptation to be a bully yourself
If it is your own group of friends who are the bullies, you are in a really tough spot. Use your own judgement about what is crossing the line. Look around your friends and see which ones

are uncomfortable with what the group is doing or planning. Be strong enough to say what you think. Voice your opinion if you think someone is being nasty or picking on someone else. Say things like, 'We're better than this,' and, 'We don't have to pick on someone just because we can.'

Be sure to walk away. Maybe other members of the group will walk away with you. Use your own judgement about how much you can influence without them turning on you. Trust your own feelings that this behaviour is going to end badly. Acknowledge that you need to do something. If you are feeling too intimidated to be able to challenge the leader in any way, then you have to ask yourself, 'Are these friends really worth being with?'

Typically, when bullying occurs in a group, there is one person trying to push their own agenda. This person bullies others into following. There is nothing worse than feeling like your peers are putting pressure on you to do things you know are wrong. If you see something really disturbing, you need to think carefully about how you can help without putting yourself at risk. Talk privately to one of your teachers you feel you can trust. Your parents can also help you with this by making a call to an admin member to let them know what is happening, and to ask that they are careful not to identify you. Anything is better than having to live with the knowledge that someone else got really hurt and you did nothing as a bystander.

You don't have to be friends with everyone. There are many gains in behaving in a friendly manner to everyone, even the people you don't really like. Be smart. Keep your negative opinions about others to yourself. If you do this you will find over time, as everyone matures, that you will be liked and respected. If, on the other hand, you are the one who is throwing your weight around, then you need to ask yourself what you are trying to prove. What it is that you are so unhappy about that you have to direct your anger at others? I doubt that you are a bully, because real bullies would probably not bother to read this paragraph!

- If you are a bystander, find a safe way to report.
- Be strong enough to try to dissuade others from bullying.
- Walk away, demonstrate you will not be part of it.
- Look around for others who feel the same.
- Reassess if this is really the group of friends you want.

1.3. Does your teacher have it in for you?

It is quite common for students to feel disliked by a teacher. Sometimes it can feel like you have got off on the wrong foot, and other times you simply don't know the cause. It is always frustrating if you don't know why a person doesn't seem to like you. Often it comes down to a misunderstanding – like all human beings, teachers are not perfect. While a teacher might enjoy the company of one student more than another, just as you do, a professional teacher will be fair to all students. Remember though that teachers can get things wrong. They can have bad days, too.

At the end of the day, teachers go home to their families and they sit up late at night preparing lessons for their classes. Teachers usually enter the profession because they want to make a difference and help kids prepare for life. If, through your behaviour, you make your teacher's job harder, you can expect your teacher will be annoyed with you. That doesn't mean your teacher doesn't like you. Teachers really don't even have the time to think about whether they like you or not.

Teachers are in charge of the whole class. Because they can't physically have their eyes in every place at once, they rely on evidence of what they have seen previously. Once you earn the reputation of being a talker or a troublemaker, the teacher will most likely look at you, expecting that you have been chatting. Even when you are doing the right thing, the teacher will likely get it wrong because he or she expects it to be you who is causing the problem. You can't blame the teacher if you have been guilty on many previous occasions and have earned the reputation as a talker.

If you decide to change your behaviour and want to turn a bad relationship into a better one, you will have to be patient until the old reputation fades. Don't give up! Keep trying to do the right thing and your efforts will pay off. It usually takes about three months of good behaviour for the teacher to notice and believe that you have changed your attitude. You just have to wear that. Be patient. Once you have decided to behave well your relationship with your teacher will start to improve. Your efforts will pay off.

- Teachers really don't have time to decide if they like you or not.
- If you are constantly disrupting the class, you will be the first person the teacher looks at because that is the expectation you have created.
- When you decide to behave in class, give it three months for the teacher to notice that you have changed your attitude.
- Your efforts will pay off.

1.4. Have you been acting dumb to avoid getting stirred?

In the middle years, it is quite common for the less motivated members of the class to stir anyone they perceive as smart. Don't worry about it. These stirring students are the ones with the problem. If your teacher sings your praises too much, making you a target of scorn, there are things you can do to change this. While it is not ideal for you to tone down some of the things you say in class as a solution, if you really feel you have to do this in the short-term to make your life easier, then that is okay. A better idea is to let your teacher know that you find it difficult.

You can find other ways to show your teacher that you are interested. The teacher will understand this, and may help by keeping your achievements a little more private. If you choose to opt out of class participation, say all you want to say in your head. Know exactly what you are doing and why, and know that it is temporary, or only for this class. Know that this is a form of bullying. You have to decide at what point you can or can't deal with it.

Be very careful not to take on the apathy of other students. It is silly to give power to people who don't care about their education. Remember, by the middle of Year 10, when you are flying through with good grades it will start to dawn on the unmotivated kids that you are building a successful future. They will realise that you will be choosing tough academic or vocational subjects for senior schooling, all of which lead to interesting careers. They will most likely leave school for uncertain future employment. The kids currently giving you a hard time will be viewing you with secret admiration when that time comes.

1.5. How to avoid feeling overwhelmed in Senior School

In Year 11 it is normal to feel overwhelmed. This may be the first time that you have been given a whole term or semester's workload at the beginning of the year. Heavy workloads are overwhelming and they happen every year, including post-Year 12 studies. Accept that this feeling is normal and that it will pass. Concentrate on one step at a time – the rest will follow easily if you just start.

The key to success at this level of education is to organise yourself well and to start tasks early, using the chart we discussed earlier. If you are doing an assignment the night before it is due, you can only expect an average mark for an average effort. If you start an assignment the minute you get it, you have time to work on it and have it completed in time to put it away for a day or two, then pick it up just before it is due to put the final touches on it. Refining and rewriting leads to high marks and, if you are well-organised and start early, you will not feel overwhelmed by the amount of work ahead of you. Starting early and asking for guidance are essential skills that will see you through any course you ever want to complete.

Most students love the senior years because they enjoy throwing themselves into new activities. Take the risky step of volunteering for new opportunities that come your way. If, you are feeling very lethargic and unmotivated, then check-in with yourself. Are you playing the, 'I don't care, I'm not going to try' game? The game part is a little script going on in your head that says, 'If I don't try, then no one will find out I am dumb.'

Boys in Year 11 particularly love this game. The trouble is, it is built on a fallacy of being dumb. The reality is that we are all ordinary people who often feel dumb when we don't know something. Feeling like a fraud is common when you are in a new situation where you become well aware of all you don't know. Focus on what you can learn, rather than what you don't know. Get help if you can't settle your anxious thoughts sufficiently to focus on one task at a time. Start work, step by step, do what you need to do.

If you are thinking you would rather leave school than have to sort all this out, think about the following. Throughout Australia most students complete Year 12. Finishing at the end of Year 10 or Year 11 will put you in the minority. It is not impossible to go back to complete Year 11 or 12 after you have left school, but it is hard. If you later decide you want to gain university qualifications, you will have to take a year out to do a tertiary preparation course before you can enrol. This is a big decision.

Having said that, for some students who have a solid plan of employment and some kind of ongoing training that will provide good outcomes, this might be a good solution. For instance, an apprenticeship will give you a valuable qualification and training. You may not like school, but you may enjoy a training course in an area that holds interest for you. Do not stop yourself from getting qualifications just because you don't like school.

If you prefer practical learning rather than theoretical study, an alternative pathway may be good for you. Even working or volunteering for a year with the option of returning to school later is a better scenario than just leaving. It is so important to get further training in some area after leaving school. Talk this over with your parents or significant adults around you. It is so important to plan something that will provide future training and opportunities for learning and personal growth.

- Trust in your ability. Ignore any negative thought that says 'I can't do this.'
- Settle any anxious thoughts that stop you from taking one step at a time to complete tasks.
- Never leave education without a plan for ongoing future training, opportunities for learning and personal growth.

1.6. The last year of school: an emotional time

Whether you are in the last year of school, or you are completing an apprenticeship or a training course, the time can seem both too long and too short at the same time. Partway through your last year, you won't be alone in wanting school/training to be over so you can get on with life. It is potluck as to whether you end up in a cohort of students who are generally nice and caring toward each other, or whether you end up in a group that runs down or derides other students behind their backs. Even when year groups of students are known to be unsupportive of each other, it is usually the case that, by the end of their time together, they bond as school leavers who are about to face the big wide world. In other words, they grow up.

It is natural to want to get into the adult world and be treated like the adult you know you are becoming. While you are there, try to enjoy your contact with your teachers/instructors as they regard you more and more as adults. Most teachers are genuinely concerned and willing to help you in any way. They want to send you on your way with as many skills as possible. If they give you a hard time, listen! They have most likely identified something going wrong with your attitude, your work ethic, or your willingness to have a go. If you are honest with yourself you will know if their comments are fair and accurate. Their motivation is to help you get through.

Enjoy the fun parts of your last year. Work hard when you need to work hard, and look around to connect with those friends who might potentially be friends for life. Be kind and supportive to your classmates, regardless of how they are to you, and become the kind of adult you want to be (one who is respected and liked for who you are).

With all the emotional turmoil, if you have been taking it all out on your parent/caregiver, it might be time to appreciate what they have done for you. No one is a perfect parent, but your parents have gone to work for many years, have filled the fridge, and encouraged you all the way. They have supported you financially, physically, emotionally, and mentally. One thing you probably don't appreciate at this point in time is the unconditional love that people in your life have given you. You are very lucky if you have come from a family that loves you unconditionally. This means that, regardless of all the mistakes you may have made, they are still there to support you if ever life gets really tough. This is a wonderful asset that gives you a backboard from which you can launch into your life.

As a young adult you are now in a position to commence giving this kind of unconditional love back to your parents. This means that no matter whether or not you agree with their style of parenting, their set of values, or their disciplinary actions, you can appreciate them for who they are, and the fact that they have loved and wanted the best for you from the time you were born. You might want to think about the gratitude you feel for your family or the other adults in your life who have supported you, and make amends for any hurt you may have caused. If you have not been lucky enough to have a supportive family, then pride yourself on your efforts to get through senior schooling on your own. Enjoy and celebrate your success.

- Savour your last year of school! It will go quicker than you realise.
- Do the hard yards and enjoy the fun moments.
- Be kind to all and celebrate your successes.
- Show your appreciation for all those who have supported you.
- Look forward to the world opening up new and exciting pathways.

Chapter 2

2

Friends

2.1. When friendship groups chop and change

2.2. Friendships that hurt

2.3. Being liked vs. being popular

2.4. Making close, intimate friendships

2.5. Becoming more assertive

2.6. The lure of drugs

2.7. Social media and gaming

2.8. When friends are in trouble

2.9. Dating

2.1. When friendship groups chop and change

It is great if you happen to have a group of friends who you really like and who stay together throughout school. This is rare, and there are both positives and negatives to this. The more friends you make, the more you learn about yourself and other people. Variety brings richness, and you will find that with each activity you do, whether it is a club, sport, or social activity, your social network will expand. The beauty of this is that you will start to feel more confident. Try it!

Friendship groups can also start to take on different values that cause tension. If you feel uncomfortable, fearful, or anxious, you might need to gradually distance yourself from your social group, exploring other opportunities for friendship. In school, a good trick is to leave your bag with your base group while you go and socialise with other groups. This will help you find a group you feel more comfortable with.

- Keep broadening your friendship group. Do activities outside school that provide the opportunity to make new friends.
- Changes in friendship groups are natural.
- Be mindful that your friendship group is not your whole world.

2.2. Friendships that hurt

When best friends betray you, it can be extremely devastating. When you think you have a solid friendship but your so-called friend dumps you for a different friend, or suddenly doesn't want to spend time with you, it is hard to feel philosophical about it. It hurts! When you are over the shock, stand back and ask yourself what went wrong. Was this friend the kind of person who doesn't like to say no, and follows anyone who sways them? Are they nice to your face but different when talking with someone else?

It takes a while to acquire a network of good friends. It can take years to find tried and true friends who will stick by you, and always be kind. If everything is going wrong in your social group and you are really unhappy, just do a little internal check. Have you been mean in any way? If it is a group of people that are making you feel left out, have a think about which person in the group is the ringleader. Groups generally have just one or two self-elected leaders, people who sweep others along with them.

What about the other group members? Think about the group dynamics. Are there some who stay in the background? Is it possible they feel as you do? If so, it might be worth gradually getting to know them better. Strength can be gained from others who feel the same as you do.

Perhaps there is a family member, or someone you have regular contact with who really gets to you, who leaves you feeling hurt or upset. Try and work out what sort of person they are. Does this person have a need for constant praise or attention? Do they want to dominate, or be better than everyone else? Are they the jealous kind, oversensitive, or always wanting to make things about them? Is this person angry a lot, or constantly unhappy? Does this person resent the way you get along with someone else? Does this person put you down or demean you just to show that they are more dominant, more important, or more powerful? Are they nasty to everyone?

When someone doesn't like you, it can often be more about them than you. As long as you are being kind and considerate of their feelings, then you can step back and say to yourself, 'I can't do it any more, this person has his/her own problems to sort out.'

More practically, if someone is really mean to you the best thing you can do is turn your back and walk away. No one gains from tolerating nasty or unkind behaviour. It is better to spend lunchtimes in the library than be with a group of mean people. If it is hard to escape nasty students, it is often possible to request a class or grouping change. Talk to your parents if you are really unhappy or feel powerless to do anything about it. They will help you work something out. Life is too short to be miserable, and there is always a solution to be found. Remember, there are so many nice, kind, and respectful people in this world that it is silly to stay stuck in a group that is mean.

> - It is better to spend lunchtimes in the library than be with a group of mean and nasty so called 'friends'.
> - Trust your own wisdom about how friends should treat each other.
> - Take time to find true friends and cherish them when you find them.

2.3. Being liked vs. being popular

There is always a 'popular' group, a 'cool' group who set themselves up to be the envy of other students. They act like they are the only people in the school who are important. If you have had thoughts of wanting to be in this group, think carefully. These groups are often made up of uncaring people who look down on others. Being liked and respected for who you are and what you stand for is a much better way to go, rather than trying to impress this group.

If things are going wrong and you are finding it hard to make good friends, there may be some things you are doing that push other people away, even though this is not what you want to happen.

You can inadvertently push others away by

- acting bored all the time, and doing every chore like it is a huge effort.
- chasing after friendships, desperate to make new friends rather than waiting for them to come to you.
- being a killjoy when your friends want to have a bit of fun by being silly.
- putting down other people's ideas – putting a block on other people's enthusiasm.

- taking but never giving – expecting others to help you but never getting around to returning the favour.
- treating others like they don't deserve you.
- playing subtle games or misrepresenting what others say for your own gains.
- talking about yourself all the time or being selfish.
- taking too long when you ask questions or explain something.
- using sarcasm when talking about someone else's ideas.
- whinging and being negative all the time – acting hard done-by.
- mucking other people around by being indecisive or keeping them waiting.
- blaming others and turning things around so it is never your fault.
- always having to go one better than your friends – trying to be superior in every way.

> - Be liked and respected for who you are and what you stand for.
> - If you feel you have to impress to gain a friend, this may not be the right friend for you.
> - Take stock of how you treat others.

2.4. Making close, intimate friendships

Strangely, you are most likely to attract new friends when you are relaxed and being yourself. Instead of trying to twist into becoming someone you think others will like, just have a go at liking yourself. If you are one to compare yourself to others then you are on a very dangerous pathway to destroying your self-esteem. Look beyond yourself and focus on making others happy instead.

Challenge your thinking. Value your attributes. Address any part of yourself you don't like and compliment it on what it has done for you. Remember, having a fantastic body does not make people happy. Highly-attractive women will often say they want to be admired for their brain, not their body. They want to be loved for the person they are, rather than be a trophy for someone. You are who you are, and comparing yourself to others only puts you into a false world of thinking the grass is greener on the other side. Most likely, this is quite untrue. Focus on who you are and what you can bring to this world.

Work at putting others at their ease and be kind to everyone. If you are relaxed and ready to have a good laugh, you will find others will flock to be in your company. It is when people try to be someone or something they are not that problems arise. If you are genuine and behave in ways that help you like yourself, sooner or later you will meet friends who are the same.

There are many ways to make others feel comfortable in your presence:

- Congratulate them and be supportive of their efforts.
- Smile and use the person's name — listen to their interests and look them in the eye.
- Realise that everyone needs to feel valued and appreciated.
- Remember special things about them; ask them about things they have mentioned to you, like the name of their dog, or where they were going on holidays.
- Be sincere, rather than fake.
- Tell your friends you appreciate what they do for you — 'thanks' and 'sorry' should be ready parts of your vocabulary.
- Be sufficiently confident in yourself to let others know what you think and how you feel; agree to differ in opinion.
- Be cheerful – a smile costs nothing and it will gain you a reputation as someone who is approachable.

- Be a good listener and never blab about what someone tells you in private.
- Avoid being two-faced.

Choose carefully the friends you allow closest to your heart. Not everyone can be trusted with your feelings. Don't rush into telling a new friend everything. Take time to observe how they treat other people's secrets — it can be devastating in a school situation when someone blows your trust and spreads information you don't want shared. When you eventually find a true friend who you know you can always trust, you will probably find that person will become a lifelong friend.

Above all, understand that really good friends don't come along every day. When you are feeling lonely it is tempting to seek out new friends and go overboard in accommodating their wishes. Constantly seeking affirmation for the friendship tells others that you are more interested in your own needs than simply liking them. There is no point in really chasing after people to affirm your friendship. Be patient, wait to find the people who will like you for who you are.

Make priority for friends who make you a priority. It is easy to have lots of friendships that are superficial or casual, but you only find really close friends a few times in your life, and they need to be cherished. Don't let conflict get in the way of a close friendship continuing. Conflict is normal because people have different opinions. Agree to disagree, without holding grudges. Forgive and ask for forgiveness.

Try something like this: 'I'm sorry I got so heated about [the situation]. I have thought about your point of view and I don't want our friendship to suffer just because we don't quite think the same.'

A little humility never hurt anyone — it is what makes a relationship thrive. When you show humility and forgiveness, most decent people will reflect on their own behaviour and acknowledge that they, too, may have stepped over the line.

> - Be careful who you trust with your personal information, especially in a school setting.

2.5. Becoming more assertive

Bullies will appear all throughout your life. They can shout, interrupt, put people down, ridicule, or relish in sending up others. It is not pleasant having to deal with someone who is aggressive. If you respond passively it means acting like a doormat – letting everyone walk over you. You apologise, give in, and put yourself down. This may allow the conflict to pass by but, in the process, you have sold yourself short and lost some self-respect.

If you respond aggressively this means shouting, demanding, ridiculing, or accusing. It says that you want your own way at all costs. This simply fuels conflict and encourages more hostility. Unless the other person becomes passive and gives in, you are still unlikely to get your needs met.

If you respond assertively it looks quite different to a passive or an aggressive response. It means that you confidently stand up for yourself and state what you think, feel, and prefer to happen. When you are assertive you are neither being a doormat nor an abuser. Assertive people have their needs met more frequently than those who behave passively or aggressively. When you put your preferences out in an assertive manner it is highly likely that they will be met.

It is good to take a stand, saying what you think and what you want or prefer to happen. Even though you are standing up for yourself, you are still showing respect towards the other party, as you ask for what you want. Stand tall, make direct eye contact, and clearly state what you would prefer using 'I' language. For instance, 'I think that is one possibility, but you know, I would prefer to do [X],' or, 'I think it a much better idea to do [Y].'

You also need to know how you feel about the situation, though you might choose not to talk about this. If you ask yourself internally what it is you are feeling, it will give you a good guide to what you really want to happen. For instance, if you are really feeling hurt, this might lead you to ask for an apology.

Being assertive takes practice. To start with, just notice how often you don't put yourself forward and change that around. Instead of saying, 'I don't mind,' make a decision. Be positive, too. Say, 'Yes, I would like to go to the pool,' or, 'I'd prefer honey on my toast.' If you're worried, practise on family first.

Next, give someone a compliment, express an opinion, or ask someone for help. Show affection for someone, tell them when you feel angry, or let someone know you don't appreciate being criticised. State your right and express your need. Strike up a conversation with someone you don't know. These are all ways to exercise being assertive.

Be on the lookout for power struggles
If there is a bit of rivalry in your group or class situation, be alert to 'power plays'. Is someone just trying to show who is boss by drawing you into conflict? Try to avoid getting sucked into that kind of battle. Be gracious, but decline. Point out the good parts of their ideas, then follow up with some problem-solving. Gradually introduce your idea in a slightly different way. Use influence, rather than power. People hung up on power often feel they have to dominate and shout down others. Look for ways to have your voice heard.

If there is a complete disagreement between something you want and something they want, then strike a bargain: 'Okay, let's go your way this time and my way next time.' If, when next time comes and they are not willing to give you your choice, then walk away. Ask yourself if these friends are good friends.

The art of managing conflict is to come up with a creative solution. This might include

- making sure you listen well so the other person feels heard.
- letting the other person save face.
- not stepping on another person's ego.
- asking questions rather than ordering someone around.
- admitting when you get it wrong and apologising.
- encouraging others when they achieve and praising what has worked well rather than focusing on mistakes.
- leading by example and matching your actions to your words – practicing integrity.

Power struggles will sometimes tempt you to really stand your own ground as a matter of principle. Hostility breeds hostility. It is easy to get drawn into argument. You might find yourself in situations where this causes you a huge dilemma. It might mean a choice of giving into peer pressure or losing friends. This is not a nice situation to be in because you will have to decide whether the friends are really worth backing down on what you want. Again, try to find creative ways to get your point across.

Try not to be sucked into the kind of peer pressure where you feel you have to have the latest app or iPhone, or the newest clothes. Be your own person with your own values rather than be sucked into materialism.

Know the difference between what you want and what you need. What you want is always going to be a priority list for the future. You can work towards what you want, but if you indulge too much you may find you do not have what you really need. Be assertive and stand up for your right to think what you think, but make sure you don't put others down when you state your case.

- Be alert to people hung up on power who love to 'shout down' others.
- Be assertive. Say what you think, feel, and prefer to happen.

2.6. The lure of drugs

From my experience, the kinds of kids who are attracted to drugs are often those who are somewhat introverted. They are often worriers who feel anxious about everything. Some say they take drugs to help them forget about their worries and to bring themselves out of their shell. Others say they just wish to explore, being keen for an adventure into new, but dangerous territory.

Understand that the whole drug cycle works like this: the seller befriends you first, then enthuses you by telling you things that make you curious. They might give you fake facts about side effects, or maybe some freebies. They will be super friendly, even if you are much younger. Nicknames for dangerous drugs make them sound less serious. There is always something new in the market that has a catchy name and is purported to be harmless. The seller entices you to just try it, saying there is no harm. The seller pesters you, expecting you to give in. Once the seller has you liking it, money changes hands. Your money goes to the seller. Victory – the seller gets richer and you get the problem.

The tricky thing is that the seller is not necessarily a big awful stranger, but may be one of your friends, maybe someone you have known since kindergarten, or maybe even the parent of one of your good friends. The seller is usually very friendly and helpful until you become reliant, dependent, or addicted to the substance. It is hard to argue because the substance makes you feel really good until it starts to go out of your system. Hitting stark reality is a big come down; your body starts to crave the good feeling again. The cycle repeats and gets stronger until you are finding you want it every day.

Without use, your body cries out for the drug. You become more anxious and agitated, or extremely depressed. The seller then stands back and puts pressure on you for more money to give you more stuff. You become no more than another source of income to the seller, and end up with a major problem. Methamphetamine-laced drugs are particularly seductive because they increase your dopamine in your brain making you feel really on top of everything, and give you a false confidence that you could say no to the drug at a moment's notice. They seduce you, and you feel great until you reach a sort of tipping point where the craving is so strong you start to behave in crazy ways, and your rational perspective changes. The neurons just don't fire in the same way as previously.

There is no point talking about individual drugs here because the rate of change is phenomenal. There are always new ones. Think carefully before allowing yourself to be sucked in to this kind of cycle. If you make a mistake and become seduced into the cycle, ask for help as soon as possible. You do not have to deal with this alone. Keeping it secret is only furnishing the drug dealer's pockets with cash.

It is important to know your facts about the effect of drugs. Look at the latest research on various drugs and alcohol, find out which ones are illegal, and know the risks associated with each kind of drug. Note in particular the risks for psychotic events and the risks of ongoing psychiatric illness or deepening addictions. At the time of writing, there is mounting evidence of strong links between adolescent use of THC and psychosis, and a higher likelihood of developing schizophrenia 10 years down the track. Most of the young people I know who have been sucked into the drug cycle in a serious way have been left with major anxiety issues that are far worse than prior to drug-taking. This kind of future is not what you want.

Drugs are largely an unknown quantity. How they take effect will vary from person to person. I dislike drugs of all kinds because even some legal drugs used for medical reasons can sometimes cause more damage than good. I know that there is nothing I can write here to persuade you about what to think about drugs – you will make up your own mind.

If you know you are anxious and looking to drugs for relief, know that there are lots of other ways you can learn to manage your overthinking. Everyone in the world has anxious thoughts, it is part of living. How you process those thoughts and your ability to switch into the here and now is the part that you have to learn so that you can handle all kinds of situations. You will be happier in yourself, and you won't need to get into drugs just to get by.

Experimenting with drugs can be dangerous if you are not in a safe environment where someone will look after you should you have a bad reaction – like anything, risks need to be assessed and safety plans need to be in place. Approximately 1/5 of people have bad psychotic reactions to certain drugs. These can sometimes last a lifetime. If you do choose to take a drug, look at the environment around you and judge the safety of where you are, and who you are with.

Make your own decisions and avoid just being swept along by a group of friends. The really scary thing is that there will be a proportion of your whole group of friends who go on to be habitual drug users. This may cause them to miss out on their secondary and tertiary qualifications, and they are more likely to lose years out of their life. If these friends do live through their habit, when they finally take stock of their lives and the life they have lost, they usually regret ever having anything to do with drugs. I have heard it many, many times.

If you choose to explore alcohol, then be sensible about what, where, and how. Take each drink slowly, wait to see how it affects you before you take the next. Make sure you have eaten, and keep eating while you drink. Drink water, as well. Make sure you are with mates who will look after you, Take turns in being the one to be absolutely sober in case someone needs to be cared for. Don't be fooled; alcohol is also a drug that can have addictive properties for some people. Watch any mates who appear too keen to get drunk on a regular basis.

The problem with any kind of drug, legal or illegal, is that there is a point at which you can lose control over your body, your behaviour, and your perceptions. I have counselled countless young people who have ended up in hospital, who have been sexually assaulted, or have engaged in behaviour they have later regretted. Losing control of yourself in any situation puts you at risk.

> - Losing control of yourself in any situation puts you at risk.
> - Be well-informed and wise about the risk associated with any substance use.

2.7. Social media and gaming

Let's think about the basics of friendship. A friend is someone who knows you, your family, the kind of life you lead, the morals you hold, your likes and tastes. A friend sees you in context with other friends, teachers, or sporting team members. A friend supports you through rough times. A friend forgives temporary misunderstandings, and a good friend takes responsibility to apologise and avoid repeating a mistake. A friend goes out of their way to engage in activities they know you will enjoy. Friends think of you first, before themselves.

Social media brings many other dynamics that should not be confused with real friendship. Like many good things in life, a moderate amount has many benefits but too much social media can be harmful. Social media teaches you to be self-absorbed and needing constant positive feedback. In checking for how many 'likes' on your post, or how many birthday wishes you get, you are priming yourself to be always looking for positive affirmation. A lack of likes or comments can result in some people feeling quite down and depressed.

While you're young, your family and friends freely give you gifts and money. In the adult world, you have to be very cautious about anyone who wants to give you something, or wants to meet up with you to get to know you. Be highly suspicious of anyone who wants to give you something for nothing. Regrettably, this rarely happens with good motivation in the adult world.

Be careful not to be sucked into social media scams. With social media and online gaming, there are trolls who take delight in ridiculing or criticising others. They post nasty or obscene comments that are designed to hurt you in some way. The stranger-danger lessons you had in Grade 1 apply just as much to social media as anywhere else. Be very wary of strangers in person or on the internet. Be aware that there are undesirable people on the internet trying to trick you into thinking they are your very best friend. Paedophiles are skilled criminals who have deception and manipulation down to a fine art in ways you would never believe possible. It is easy to fool yourself that the people you are playing with are your friends when they may be financial, emotional, or sexual predators.

Be careful. Only play interactively with friends you already know well. Never give away personal details and always ask yourself the question, 'Would my parents approve of what I am doing?' Never give out any information like your name, where you live, or where you go to school unless you check with your parent or caregiver first. It is not just a case of using your common sense. Many social engineering tricks are designed to not raise any alarms with your common sense. It is best to have the policy of not trusting anyone you meet on the internet; never agree to meet up with anyone you have met online.

There are other aspects of social media that cause concern. When you crouch over hand-held devices, or produce high adrenalin while playing games or other activities, you hold your body in a physical state that simulates anxiety. Continually hunching triggers the physical aspects of anxiety, like forgetting to breathe properly. Headaches from lack of oxygen can result and you can easily develop a long-term problem with a range of anxiety symptoms that persist even when you are not using the device.

Social media can stop you from connecting with a world bigger than yourself. You will have seen classic photos or situations where everyone is on their hand-held device rather than being present at the party or gathering they are attending. Social media takes your time away from interacting and giving to others. It can take time away from you achieving your own goals.

In addition to this, there is often a level of competition that goes on with social media. It's important to not fall into the trap of trying to collect as many friends as you can. Be a little more prudent because there is a difference between connecting with true friends with whom you have shared experiences, and just connecting with a name for the sake of boosting your numbers! The latter can be dangerous and hollow.

When you play games online, it is essentially a selfish pleasure. You play because of what you get out of it. You play at your own convenience, to fulfil your own need for entertainment. You might gain computer game skills, and you might learn those from others. You might have a joke with your online friends. All this might be enjoyable, but remember that online friends can disappear instantly unless they are real friends you see every day. With purely online friendship there is no kindness or caring for the other, just a whole lot of people doing something for personal entertainment. Be careful not to confuse this kind of friendship with real friendship.

It is good to have different friends in different contexts, friends who share your interests. You can have a group of friends in a sporting club, and another group of friends in a chess club or a drama club. We see those people only when we do those activities. They are not close friends, but we are friendly with them in those contexts. We can at least see them and probably know people who know them well. Again, this is different to purely online friendships with strangers we know nothing about.

Even when you play with people you know through school or sporting clubs, you need to think about whether the amount of time spent is excessive. If it is, think about what you might be doing if you were not playing games online. It may be that online gaming is taking you away from interacting with your friends in a broader and more satisfying way. It might be that this kind of play is taking priority over healthier activities where your friends may be able to take on different roles. You might enjoy different strengths in yourself and friends that you may never have been aware of because of the narrow roles created by the structure of the gaming.

Social media and online gaming can become quite addictive. Especially with gaming, your mind craves the excitement that is anticipated. Away from gaming, life can seem flat and boring because there is a lack of targeted stimulation being thrown at you. If you have withdrawn from friends and activities you might also experience a loss of identity, a sense that you have nowhere to belong other than with your online friends. That environment skilfully draws you back in. The neurons in your brain are ready for the stimulation, and the neural pathways are strong and ready for use. They drag you there with great force.

Developers of games are experts in providing the kinds of cues to keep you engaged. They are highly-skilled in providing reward stimuli that keeps you hooked into playing the game. The ego boosts that come with points, rebellions, and privileges are hard to resist. On physical, mental, and emotional levels you start to crave the stimulation that comes with gaming. I have known many young men who have fallen prey to online gaming that has consumed two or more years of their lives. Their sleep structure is damaged as they stay up all night to communicate with players on the other side of the world. They become unable to cope with normal daily activities.

With some caution around the above issues, if you wish to engage in interactive gaming, do so with the strict principle that it is a fantasy world that should be kept very separate from reality. Stay away from online strangers. Be wary of any kind of demand made of you or your time, because this demand comes from an environment where there is no real commitment to friendship. Understand that increasing demands on your time can suck up the energy you might otherwise have for the rest of your life, where you are likely to make true, lifelong friends, as well as achieve your goals. Just as you might limit your time for hobbies, sport, or socialising, make sure you limit your time for online gaming interactions. If you fail to do this you will find yourself living in a world that does not really exist past the tap of a computer keyboard.

- Social media teaches you to be self-absorbed and to need constant positive feedback.
- Social media can stop you from experiencing real connection with real friends.
- Stay away from strangers online and those who offer you something for nothing.
- Never give out personal information or arrange to meet an online stranger.

2.8. When friends are in trouble

Friendships can, at times, be quite demanding. When your friend is emotionally upset it is inevitable that you will feel something similar, even if there is nothing going wrong in your life. Make sure you take stock of all the things you are grateful for in your life and remind yourself that this is your friend's journey, not yours.

It is easy to diminish our own lives by getting swept up in the troubles that belong to other people. That does not mean you should lack empathy or be uncaring, but that you should keep a boundary around your own life and emotions. You can still do many things to help your friends. By staying strong and keeping your own personal boundaries you will be able to be more helpful. Understand that you can't lead someone else's life for them; what you can do is empower your friend to do what they need to do to manage their own life.

How might your friends be in trouble?
Maybe your friend's family situation is not great, or your friend is not physically well. Maybe your friend discloses sexual abuse. Whatever personal details your friend shares with you, understand that it is an honour that they trust you sufficiently to open up to you. Being able to share our deeper hurts is really important for all of us.

Let your friend know that you care. Be patient and listen carefully. Once your friend has shared something personal with you they may feel quite vulnerable, so reassure them that you find it an honour to have been told. You don't have to rush in and fix the problem, just be with them and attend to their needs.

If someone is being abused or is suicidal, it is an impossible request to ask you to hold their secret. With sexual abuse (something that is an illegal act), there is a higher level of morality that comes into play. You have to explain that because you care for them you want the bad stuff to stop happening – that you want them to feel safe. Your friend will be in a state of fear and unable to see the bigger picture, and this is really tough, but you need to tell your friend that you need to get some adult or professional help. Ask them their preference about who you might approach, but explain that you can't hold their secret because that means perpetuating the abuse that is happening, that it needs to stop immediately. If you fail to tell someone, you are essentially condoning the ongoing abuse.

With issues where the abuse happened in the past and your friend is not currently at risk, then you can take a little time to convince your friend to see a counsellor. Maybe you can offer to go with them if they feel hesitant. Explain that you don't have professional skills and that your friend needs the very best care.

At the other end of the spectrum, if your friend continually unloads emotional issues on you, is content to receive lots of care and sympathy from you but refuses to seek assistance from a counsellor, parent, or the law, you will need to think hard about what to do. In this scenario, your friend lacks self-responsibility, and may be playing an attention-getting game. It is not fun to be on the receiving end of this. It can be too hard for anyone to deal with ongoing misery unless they have been trained to do so, and it doesn't serve the person well to not have anything change in their life. Explain how you feel and encourage them to attend a counselling session to start the process of dealing with the issues. If this person refuses assistance and comes up with every excuse under the sun, then you need to be careful about how much emotional energy you use on their behalf.

Step back. Let your friend know you care about them but, at the same time, let them know that you can't help them if they are not prepared to help themselves. This sounds harsh, but it is an important boundary that needs to be reinforced, for both their sake and your own. To stay in the constant state of powerlessness is not good for your friend. It is also not good for you to have a shadow of sadness constantly over your life while all the good aspects of living pass you by.

- You can't lead someone else's life for them.
- Helping means empowering others to do for themselves.
- When someone is being harmed or is suicidal they lose their right to confidentiality.

2.9. Dating

When you meet someone you really like, it is important to spend time with that person without the pressure of any kind of classification like 'a first date'. Do something that you both enjoy. This might be something sporting, cultural, or social. Meet up with friends for a particular event, or choose somewhere where you can both feel safe and comfortable.

Pick somewhere where there are other people around, or where you can go on public transport. Take your phone and stay away from places where there is alcohol or drugs. When you meet someone for the first time, it is common not to know very much about them, so put yourself in their position. Imagine how your outing might feel in an environment that is potentially unsafe. Consider their need to be able to relax and feel safe.

Plan to have fun. Laughter and fun activities will make your friendship grow quickly. Be aware that there can also be different expectations about what kind of intimacy might occur. Make sure that you communicate the kind of environment you are suggesting the two of you will visit. Put your friend's mind at ease that you are not proposing a secluded place where he or she might worry that there will be expectations of sexual intimacy. It is always a good idea to let a third person know when and where you will be going, and who you will be with.

Take time to get to know your new friend. A simple request like, 'May I hold your hand?' or, 'May I put my arm around you?'

is always the safest way to go. Take your time. Who knows? You may find that after one or more outings that this person is really not for you, that you have no interests in common. Alternatively, it could be the beginning of a long friendship.

As you get to know your friend, talk through expectations about sexual intimacy when the situation seems right. It might be that neither of you are looking for a full-on relationship, just a chance to have some fun with a good friend. Never assume from your sexual encounter that your date wants full sexual intimacy. Whatever stage your friendship is at, sexual intimacy always needs prior discussion and consent. The main thing is to talk about what you both want. This builds trust and gives you a way forward that can be relaxed and stress-free for both.

- Laughter and fun make friendships grow quickly.
- Sexual intimacy always needs prior discussion and consent.

Chapter 3

3

Starting Work

3.1. Your first job interview

3.2. What does it mean to be treated with dignity?

3.3. How to deal with a difficult boss

3.4. Bullying in the workplace

3.5. Knowing your rights

3.6. Having fun at work

3.1. Your first job interview

When you go for your first job interview, make sure you look smart. Try a little colour on you, e.g. a shirt, tie, scarf, or necklace that stands out and makes you look bright and cheery. Try rehearsing the interview in your head. You could always video yourself answering some questions to get an idea of what you look like, or you could get someone to roleplay an interview. At your first interview it feels very strange to have someone asking you direct and serious questions. Before your interview, read up on whatever you can find. Ask questions from others in similar jobs. If you are unsuccessful know that it is probably because there was a large number of applicants, rather than you 'failing' at the interview. Every interview you do will give you experience. Keep applying. Sooner or later you will find work.

The first day of a new job can feel scary. In fact, most adults report that it is. This scary feeling is normal. When confronted with any new situation our brains swing into hyperactivity and start to sift through anxious thoughts. If you look around your new workplace, you will see many young people really enjoy their casual job. There is every chance you will enjoy it, too. At the very least, you will probably like having some independent income. So, push those anxious thoughts aside and focus on how you wish to deal with this new situation. I suggest you take every opportunity to smile appropriately at everyone you meet. This will show that you are keen to be there.

If you are lucky, your first few jobs will be with employers who treat their young recruits well. Good employers provide systematic training, support, and encouragement. Remember, they will not expect you to get everything right on the first day! They know you are learning, so you need not be afraid that you will stuff up. When learning anything new, you will inevitably make mistakes – that is how you will learn. Once the mistake is evident to you, it is important that you don't keep making it over and over. Employers are not like teachers. You might think your teachers are tough on you, but the workplace is a whole new ballgame. You have be tough and able to take criticism when you do something that is not ideal. There is no wriggling out of the things you need to do. You are being paid to do what the employer tells you to do.

Take everything one step at a time. Listen carefully, follow instructions, and ask when you are not sure. If you are feeling a little nervous, just say to yourself that it is to be expected, and then put that feeling aside. Have the confidence to ask when you don't know something. You will be admired as a good employee if you are prepared to listen, learn, and ask. You may also need to accept that your trainer may not be perfect. Whatever the situation, make the best of it. Accept that everyone has limitations, but can be appreciated for the things they do well.

Know that when you step in the door, you are already valuable as an employee because you are keen to learn. A lot of time has been put into recruiting you, and your employer will want you to be successful. If you bring a happy disposition to the workplace you will be appreciated. As you gain confidence and they get to know you, many of your loved qualities will be evident.

You may have insights that others don't have. If you have a suggestion, put it to your supervisor in a way that is respectful. Say something like, 'What would you think about doing [X] this way?' or, 'I don't know if this is a crazy idea but what if…?'

Be careful never to criticise a fellow worker or boss behind their back. The workplace is different from school. You can chatter all you like amongst your friends, but in a workplace everything you say is under scrutiny, and can be reported. Keep negative comments to yourself and your trusted friends outside work.

Always remember that, regardless of age or experience, your manager should be treated with respect. Similarly, your manager should treat you with dignity and respect. Workplaces are different to other social groups. In hospitality work, in particular, you might find that you are placed under a young manager the same age as yourself. It is important to still treat that person with respect.

- It is normal to feel anxious on the first day of your new job.
- Learn from your mistakes and be prepared to take criticism.
- Keep negative comments about other staff to yourself.

Dating in the workplace

Dating can go wrong in many ways. At any time each party could find out that the other is not the right person to continue a relationship with. This can be very problematic in a work environment where it is impossible to avoid seeing that person on a daily basis. Not everyone is honourable. Hurt and bitterness can lead some people to become very nasty. They may even want to lash out, hurt, or demean someone who has broken up with them. This is vindictive behaviour.

Dating workmates can be problematic if the friendship sours. If there is a huge personal impact, it may cause one of you to have to leave the workplace. It is always safer to keep dating relationships away from work.

- Dating someone from your workplace is not a good idea.

3.2. What does it mean to be treated with dignity?

If you are dependable (show up on time), have pride in your work, show respect and consideration for others, and remain honest and enthusiastic, you will be highly valued by your employer. Whether or not you are appreciated says more about the employer. Not every young manager is skilled enough to understand the importance of making employees feel valued. In pressured workplaces, you can expect that your manager may be blunt and direct, giving you orders, and maybe even expressing some frustration because of a stressful situation, or because you haven't got it quite right. All you can do under those circumstances is listen carefully to instructions and do your best.

Try not to react to the stress. Instead, make allowance for it and think about how you could do the job better. Think of high pressure jobs like a stressful family situation where, for example, a parent has five minutes to get family members packed and out the door to catch a plane. Tempers can rise. There is pressure to know what needs to be done quickly. In high-stress situations, the best you can do is to take one step at a time and be efficient as you work.

People getting stressed and bombarding you with instructions is one thing; having someone screaming at you, calling you stupid, or belittling and demeaning you is another. This behaviour, whether in front of others or in private, is simply not on. It is not okay to broadcast to other employees when you make a mistake. This is not respectful behaviour because it robs the employee of dignity. It reflects more on the poor management skills of the person in charge than the individual's lack of skill.

Sometimes nasty people play power games or try to make you look bad through dishonest tricks. This is also not on. Hopefully this will never happen to you, but if it does, step back emotionally. Don't let it get to you, because this person is not worth worrying about. Maintain your own dignity, and don't lower yourself to the other employee's bad behaviour. This is critical. A tricky part of their power play can be to get you to behave badly, then heap the bad consequences on you.

Be smart and keep your reactions private. Go home and talk to someone you are close to. Think smart about collecting evidence and planning strategies to deal with the situation to produce a positive outcome. Take action yourself. Discourage anyone at home from stepping in for you.

Quietly and calmly collect evidence. Take note of who else might have seen or heard the situation play out. Your first action might be to let the abusive person know that you are ready to report their behaviour unless they pull their head in and start treating you with respect. Be patient; this person is bound to trip themselves up sooner or later.

If you are not feeling good enough, think about why that is. Are you struggling to do your job efficiently? Do you need more training? Remember, it is the employer's job to train you adequately, to treat you with respect, and to preserve your dignity when you do make a mistake. They must be clear about what is needed from you. If what your employer tells you does not make sense, or you do not understand, make sure you ask for clarification. Look around for another person who might be able to help you. At the end of the day, you need to walk out the door knowing you have put in good effort and have conscientiously tried to take everything in. It will get easier over time.

There is major lifelong learning in all of the above. I am not suggesting that you avoid reflecting on your own weaknesses, or that you avoid responsibility for things you do wrong. While you should always examine your own behaviour for flaws, it is also important to examine the quality of the management skills held by those in charge of you. Be honest with yourself, and trust yourself. If poor management has produced this situation, then protect your self-esteem from any blow that is coming your way.

- If you are dependable, have pride in your work, show respect and consideration for others, are honest and enthusiastic, you will be highly valued by your employer.
- NEVER EVER allow poor management or poor organisational culture to diminish your confidence or self-esteem!

3.3. How to deal with a difficult boss

It is in your best interest to inspire confidence in your employer in regard to your ability. So, before you decide if your boss is difficult or not, take careful stock of whether you have done anything rude, inappropriate, or careless. If so, then take responsibility to fix it. Forgive yourself for stuffing up; resolve to do better. Apologise to your employer and let them know you will work on it.

Each new day, make sure you smile and greet your employer with a, 'Good morning,' or, 'Good evening.' Be very quick to apologise if you think you have messed something up. Remember, everyone makes mistakes. The bigger the mistake, the more you are likely to learn. I don't think there are many people who have not made a mistake on the first day of their new job. The important thing is that you make sure you don't make the same mistake over and over. If this happens, then maybe your heart is not really in this job. Remember, there are more parts to an apology than the word. You have to mean it, acknowledge what you did, and then you have to set about making things as right as you possibly can.

If you have apologised for mistakes and put effort into changing what you do, and your employer is still difficult or continues to treat you badly, then you have two choices. The first is to accept that you have a very difficult boss and just let their criticisms flow over your head. This option requires that you acknowledge internally that your boss is the one with the problem and learn to ignore their tone or sarcasm as you get about your work. This option is suitable if you need to hang onto that work because the income you get from it is more important than your enjoyment of the job.

The other choice is to look for another job. Discuss this with your parents/carers in case they have other suggestions. Casual work might be hard work, but it should also be enjoyable. If that's not the case, you should at least be treated with respect. If this is not happening, then look for a better boss.

- Take responsibility for your mistakes, forgive yourself, and resolve to learn.
- Do not make the same mistake again.

3.4. Bullying in the workplace

Workplaces require that everyone pitch in and help when things get busy. Because of this, it is important not to be too precious. This means that you are able to take a bit of a joke, laugh, and enjoy a bit of social banter. If you are unsure whether this is what is going on in your workplace, or if you are being harassed, look to your feelings and ask yourself the question, 'Is this person intentionally setting out to make me feel inferior?' If so, then start documenting everything that is said or done, including the date, time, and witnesses to each incident.

The following bullying scenarios are examples of unacceptable behaviour in the workplace, whether they involve the employer or fellow employees:

- Being yelled at or having blatant rude remarks or offensive language screamed at you.
- Deliberately not passing on the information you require to do your job (for example, withholding the roster).
- Socially isolating you, or not including you in work-organised social activities.
- Put-downs, demeaning remarks, nicknames that offend or patronise.
- Deliberately giving incorrect instructions, information, or impossible tasks.

If you experience any of this, it's important to seek help. Identify who you can bring this issue to, such as a manager higher up the chain. If necessary, report to the government department that deals with fair work. There is government legislation in place to protect you from bullying, but it has to be reported if you want it to change. Understand that employers have a responsibility to train you, and also have a right to discipline you, and to give firm directions about how work is to be carried out. At the same time, while employers have the right to performance manage you, they are also expected to give you constructive feedback and guidance on how to improve your participation.

- Employers have the right to performance manage.
- Employers are also expected to give you constructive feedback and guidance on how to improve your participation in the workplace.

3.5. Knowing your rights

Most people find workplaces to be fair and equitable places, so it is unlucky if you find yourself in a workplace with a bully. If you do, some general knowledge about procedures can never go astray. It might assist you or one of your friends.

Firstly, remember that an accusation made with no respect for the truth or your reputation falls under the description of slander/discrimination. Secondly, understand that assault does not have to be physical. If you or a friend are fearful that you are in danger, then this constitutes assault. Thirdly, it is good general knowledge to know that if someone needs to report assault or harassment then that person should have a witness or support person present in any formal meeting. Similarly, anyone accused of doing the wrong thing should also take a witness or a support person to any consultation with the employer.

It is worth doing preparation for any formal meeting. Make a record of events and facts surrounding the situation. At the time of the meeting, insist on a private room rather than in hearing of other workers. Be clear about what you know. Present the facts simply and concisely. Stay calm and determined. Stand your ground.

In the case of accusation of sexual harassment or assault, it is standard practice that the harasser be interviewed in a different room. Each party must leave separately with a gap of time in between. Note that suspension of employment without pay is not usually permitted by law so, know what you are entitled to. Research the award wages for your area of work and be alert to an employer not paying the superannuation guarantee.

If there is a problem of any kind, start documenting straight away; any behaviour that is out of line, and note time, date, and those present. If your employer wants to pay you slightly higher wages without taking any tax or paying super for you, be very cautious how you handle the situation. Simply state that you would prefer payment in the regular way with tax and super taken out. It is illegal and not in your interests to accept wages under the table.

- Assault does not have to be physical.
- If you are feeling fearful that you are in danger then this constitutes assault.
- It is your right to be treated fairly, with respect and with dignity.

3.6. Having fun at work

Most young people who are lucky enough to get some casual work while at school really enjoy it. There can be many benefits, apart from earning money. There are new people to meet, new things to learn, and important social interactions to have. You will have the opportunity to get along with people you would not normally mix with. You will learn to communicate in a new, confident way, to be part of a team, and, most likely, you will be appreciated for any initiative you take.

Whatever the skill level required for your work, there are many subtle gains for you. It is hard to learn about how the commercial world works from the outside looking in; it is hard to understand the subtleties of an employer/employee relationships without being in such a relationship. Learning about expectations and consequences, feeling valued and appreciated for going the extra mile, or putting in extra effort will give you the tools to cope with more responsible employment later.

While casual work definitely has benefits, monitoring your own energy levels and your ability to juggle commitments is critical. Casual work can be tiring, and can disrupt your study if you are frequently called in for extra shifts. Employers can be unfairly demanding of your time, and this can affect your ability to study. Time for relaxation is important. Most people have to work to earn a living, so it is great if you love your work because it makes the time pass by quickly. Once work consumes your every day, then life outside work diminishes. Balance is always the key. Politely refuse if your employer is wanting too much of your time.

Much enjoyment can be gained from learning to get along with people from other backgrounds. It can be fun and enriching as you make contacts for life, and generally broaden your experience of the world. Enjoy putting other people at ease by chatting to them. Join in any of the fun activities that happen in workplaces.

Be ready for a bit of a laugh and tell others something you appreciate about them. Remember that this new group of people are just ordinary people. They have the same fears, worries, and self-doubts. Relax and just be yourself, keen and eager to learn. You will have fun.

- Be ready for a bit of a laugh and take any opportunity to affirm others.
- Relax and be yourself.
- Be keen and eager to learn.

4

Family issues

4.1. Seeking increased freedom

4.2. When your friends feel unsafe

4.3. Making your stepfamily work

4.4. Coping with siblings

4.5. Game playing

4.6. Negativity and attitude

4.1. Seeking increased freedom

Few parents recognise when their child has grown into a teenager. It happens so fast that most are caught unawares. Within a few months, it seems that kids can grow from being a primary school child to being more like a young adult in their thinking. While 12 months might seem like a long time in your life, it's not to your parents. So, be forgiving and get stuck into the task of bringing your parents up.

Look at it this way: when you are a child, your parents decide what you eat, what you do, how you dress, and where you go. They are used to you being a child. Then, suddenly, their child turns into a teenager. Your task is to show your parents how much you have grown up. Tell them what you think about things. Tell them how you feel. Be open to discussing the pros and cons of issues. Try to communicate like an adult.

Your parents need you to do this because a lot of change happens at a time when maybe you have made some questionable choices. Your parents can get confused because one minute they are dealing with someone who is making childish mistakes, and the next minute they are dealing with someone who is thinking like an adult. It is a very unclear time for them, just as much as it is for you.

Take every opportunity to show your parents that you can make responsible choices. What is all this fuss about taking responsibility? What does it mean? When you are a kid your parents take full responsibility for you in every aspect of your life, from making sure your teeth are cleaned, to getting you vaccinated. Being an adult means that you take on lots of responsibilities yourself. There are very few aspects of adult life that don't require you to be responsible. Whether it is driving on the correct side of the road, holding a door to prevent someone being hurt, or paying your tax on time. This is the adult life you are moving into.

Your parents fear that if you are unable to be responsible you will get yourself into a lot of trouble. You need to reassure them that they can trust you to do the right thing. An example of this would be to call them at an arranged time, or coming home at the time promised. If you are going into an unknown situation, take all the above into account and work out your safety plan. Reassure your parents by telling them what you would do if things started to go pear-shaped.

If you were at a party that suddenly got out of control with someone throwing things, acting aggressively, or taking illegal drugs, what would your plan be? Bring your parents up to where you are at in your thinking with all of this. Work on the solutions together. When they say no about something, ask their reasons. If they are adamant that you are not permitted to go somewhere, accept it and ask them at what age you will be able to do whatever it was you wanted. They know that by the time you are 18 you have to be fully independent and trusted to manage your own life and your own lifestyle, so remember, if they say no now, it doesn't necessarily mean no forever.

If your parents are fighting, try not to stress about it. If it is over you, then listen to the views of both parents and sort something out with them. If it is not about you, try not to catastrophise it. There is a lot more depth to relationships than occasional fights. There is no point living in fear that parents might separate. Even if this did happen, as you can see amongst your friends, it would not be the end of the world. Both your parents would be there for you because they love you and you will always be in a relationship with each of them. One day, before you know it, you will leave home and make your own life. Looking from the outside is never the same as looking from the inside of a relationship. If you are really worrying about it, talk to your parents.

Trust is like a brick wall. It is slow to build and quick to knock down. It is important that you build a wall of trust with your parents by behaving responsibly. This means remembering to ring them at the designated time, and being where you said you would be. It takes two seconds to send a text if you are moving to a different location. If you fail to do these kinds of things, your parents or caregivers will lose trust in you, and be even more vigilant in looking out for you. Be respectful about them caring for your safety. Keep that trust wall strong and your freedoms will be forever expanding.

If you do make a mistake, or are thoughtless, rather than rebelling and expressing your anger, show that you are adult. Admit your mistake and go with whatever consequence is applied. Show your parents that you regret your mistake and rebuild that trust wall, one brick at a time. Show them that you have learnt, and that you can be responsible. As you gain their trust, you will again be able to gradually stretch the boundaries of your freedom. If you blow it again with an inconsiderate act, the situation will worsen and your freedoms will be curtailed even more. Think about it! Remember, before you know it, you will be 18 and legally free to do whatever.

- Show your parents by your actions that you have 'grown up'.
- Make responsible choices.
- The 'wall of trust' is quick to knock down and very slow to rebuild.

4.2. When your friends feel unsafe

It is important to understand that everyone has a right to feel safe at home. If you find that one of your friends feels unsafe because their parents get angry, drunk, or are into drugs, reassure them that there is help that can be accessed. Work with your friend to put a safety plan in place. Ask their permission to tell your parents so that they can help if need be.

Plan with your friend where they could go if things get worse. Suggest that they obtain phone numbers of extended family members or close family friends, in order to ring them in case of an emergency. Get your friend to talk to the school counsellor, who will think very carefully about whether it is worth speaking to the parents to alert them of the impact on their teenager. Encourage your friend to call the police if either of the parents initiates threatening behaviour.

Encouragement and support is all you can do, but it will mean a lot. Until the situation resolves, your friend will appreciate some cheering up. The chances are that your friend will be neglected in other ways, too. For example, they may have no lunch money, or be lacking warm clothes. Again, speak to your parents or carers so that they can help you with this. At no stage try to take full control of the situation. Any action taken must happen with your friend's support and approval.

- If your friend is in trouble, put a safety plan in place.
- Enlist support.

4.3. Making your stepfamily work

It is not unusual for young people to dislike their new step-parent. It generally takes two years for a stepfamily to get settled into a routine and gain a sense of being a family unit. If you have a step-parent you dislike, it is important to know what it is that troubles you. Is it the step-parent as a person you do not like, or is it the fact that they are present in the family instead of your biological parent?

Family split-ups are tough on everyone. It is easy to be resentful of someone coming in to partner your father or mother, and it is hard to accept that your parents are not together anymore. I have talked with hundreds of high school students whose families have split up. They don't like going between houses midweek. They resent having to remember to cart everything to and fro. They hate it when one parent uses them as a means to pass on messages to the other parent, or drags them into disagreements with the other parent.

Other issues arise when one parent insists that the family must always include the new partner on family outings and activities. The students I have come across often wish they could just have time with Dad or Mum on their own. They want things to be the way they were, even with all the sibling rivalry and favouritism. This is because it is what they've always known. It is what they have been used to. Change is not easy.

If you feel any of these things, it is important to express them to one or both parents. If you want alone time with a parent, simply ask, 'Can we go somewhere, just the two of us? Would you like to come for a walk with me?' If your parent still insists that the step-parent be involved, just quietly say to them that you understand it is important that they join in, but that you really would like some time alone with Dad or Mum each week.

This is quite a reasonable thing to ask for, but make sure you don't turn it into emotional manipulation. Try to avoid those subtle nasty games of trying to get the message to the step-parent that they are not welcome here. By never wanting to go anywhere if the step-parent is there, you will defeat your purpose of trying to get some quality alone time. Your biological parent will see it for emotional manipulation and you most likely won't get what you really crave. Be careful of playing games where you ignore the presence of your step-parent, e.g. asking your parent to pass the salt when it is sitting right in front of your step-parent. Behave decently.

Be glad that your mum or dad has a partner to keep them happy. This will relieve you of a lot of caretaking that might otherwise fall your way. Think of it this way – in years to come, when you are wanting to go out and socialise on a Saturday night, would you be happy if your parent wanted you to stay home to keep them company? Your step-parent might be quite a blessing one day.

Your mum will always be your mum, and your dad will always be your dad. No one can take that away from you. Once you are used to your new family arrangement, you may actually find there are lots of advantages in these new arrangements. Each person in your life can enrich your world. Your step-parent may teach you things your own parent doesn't know anything about. Different activities and interests will enrich your life. Young people often find they have more activities and opportunities to look forward to, and more holiday experiences that those living with two parents.

- It generally takes two years for a stepfamily to consolidate and become a settled family unit.

4.4. Coping with siblings

Sometimes siblings act up and command all of your parents' or carers' attention. There might be a sick member of your family who needs your parents' attention, or there may be babies who come along. It is easy to have feelings that you are not getting the attention you need or deserve. The reality is that some personalities command a lot of attention because they are very outgoing, or very young, or both. This does not mean you are loved any less.

A baby sees Mum and Dad as being there for their every need. That is how babies learn and grow, through being closely connected to Mum or Dad. As babies grow into children they develop their own personalities. Some can be great fun while others can be really annoying at times. When kids become teenagers they, like the whole adult population, will have various traits some that are likeable, and some not so likeable. Your teenage brother or sister will know exactly how to annoy you; how to push your buttons. No doubt you know exactly how to push their buttons, as well? This is what being in a family is all about. Everyone learns how to get along. They learn how to cooperate and be patient and to share and help one another. Babies learn this as they grow up. They learn that they cannot be the centre of attention all the time.

If you are annoyed by your older siblings, try to avoid unnecessary conflict. Make a pact: 'I won't annoy you if you leave me alone.' If your brother or sister is intent on making your life a misery and you have had enough, then talk to your parent or caregiver. If they are going too far with their annoyance, you must speak up. Remember that any kind of physical, emotional, or sexual intimidation is not on from anyone, not even your sibling.

Abuse of any kind in the family setting has to be stopped at the earliest possible moment. This is not just a matter of getting someone else into trouble, it is also about helping the abusive person to know other ways of dealing with whatever issues are contributing to them behaving this way. Tell someone close to you about any abuse ASAP.

Jealous feelings amongst siblings are common. You don't need to feel bad about jealousy, but try to understand that these feelings have a single lens kind of focus. One of the hardest things to learn in life is that you can't be the best at everything. Just because one of your siblings is brilliant at sport, music, art, or mathematics does not mean that you are a failure because you don't share the same talent. Look for the things that you are good at. Everyone has special qualities, talents, and gifts. Sometimes they emerge later in life.

People throughout history often had their great achievements later in life. It is one thing to be successful at mathematics; it is another thing to be someone who can get along well with everyone around them, and be a really good team worker. The first might bring certificates at school. The latter is less obvious, but will continually bring rewards throughout your life. Love your own special gifts and talents, and think of your siblings as part of your team where each member complements each other. For all the years you play together as you grow up, each of you has contributed in some way to your siblings' talents. Their success is also partly yours.

Remember, parents have an innate love for each of their children and, without question, they love each of you deeply. Liking you is another matter. If you are often grumpy, irritable, or if you backchat, then the distance you feel between you and your parents may be more about them not liking your behaviour rather than seeming to love your siblings more. Think about it! As a young adult, you have to understand that this is a two-way relationship, not just parents always giving to you. You must also reach out and make them feel loved. If you pull away and won't hug your parents, or you push them away emotionally by refusing to talk to them, then you are likely to feel unloved.

Similarly, if they are saying or doing something that deeply upsets you, then speak up. Say, 'I really wish you would stop teasing me about [X]', 'or it really upsets me when you say things like that.' If they continue, keep saying, 'I did ask you to stop teasing me about [X].' Look them in the eye and tell them straight. Being adult is all about learning to have conversations that you expect to be hard, and finding out that they can be really easy once you start to get it out. There is nothing that cannot be talked about.

Families often lead complex lives, and there can be a lot of transactional things happening. For example, there may be lots of lunches to pack, or lots of cleaning to be done. Your parents may be thinking a lot about their careers, or financial changes. When people are caught up in thinking or doing, it is easy for them to miss how someone else is feeling. This does not mean that your parent doesn't love or care for you. If you are feeling lonely or unloved, take responsibility for that feeling and reach out to your parent.

Pick the right time. This is not in the middle of dinner preparations, or while Dad is doing the washing up. Ask to go for a walk, or speak to them after dinner. Tell them how you feel. If you are worried about how they might react to you, then start with something like, 'I know this might seem silly, but I feel [X] …,' or, 'I'm worried you won't take me seriously, or you will think I am really mean if I tell you something.' Whenever you are worried about saying something, state your worry upfront. It really helps!

Families can go through really tough times when any member of the family is really ill. It is easy to feel left out, uncared for, or even a little jealous. This then makes you feel bad because you know the family member is really sick. It is understandable that you feel angry because life is different for you. Remember, it is never fun for anyone to be sick. When life gets restricted because of illness, the ill person misses out on all sorts of things. Always ask yourself honestly, 'Who has the worst deal here?'

Try to keep your distress in proportion and know that you are angry because underneath you are really hurting for all kinds of reasons. You might be hurting because there is less time for you, or hurting because you are worried about your sick brother or sister, or simply hurting because you are confused about what is happening in your family. You can feel hurt when you see a loved one hurting. You can feel sad because life has changed and is not like it was before, or because life isn't as much fun as it used to be. These are all normal emotions to have in difficult life situations, and they deserve expression. Most likely, your parents will be feeling something similar. Let someone know how you are feeling and try not to feel guilty about how you feel. Remember, hugs help everyone.

> - Love your own special gifts and talents and think of your siblings as a team that complements each other and works together.
> - Your family is your best support when things go wrong, so treat them with respect.
> - Cuddles help everyone!
> - TELL SOMEONE CLOSE TO YOU ABOUT ANY ABUSE ASAP!
> - Being an adult is learning to have hard conversations that are inevitably easy once you 'get it out'.

4.5. Game playing

Families get to know each other extremely well. You will know each other's likes, dislikes, foibles, fears, and vulnerabilities. You will know in detail all the things that get your parents going, all the things that will drive them to argument and anger. When people play games, they use this intimate knowledge to their own advantage. For instance, you might engage in the age-old game of stitching up your brother or sister to get them into trouble for something they did not do. It might seem funny at the time, particularly on the first or second occasion, but if you continue this kind of game it may escalate and encourage your sibling to develop deeper feelings of disgust and disrespect that don't go away. There has to be an understanding that when either of you say, 'Stop, enough' that the other one takes heed. Only then can you truly have fun together.

There are many families where siblings have great relationships with their brothers and sisters. They support each other in rough times, have special fun times together, travel together, and sometimes even live together in their adult life. They get along with each other. There are also families where grown up siblings do not talk to each other because of events that occurred during their childhood. They really don't like each other because they have lost respect for each other. When there is lack of respect and caring between siblings it blows the possibility of good future relationships.

You can choose how you want to be with your siblings. You can choose to be honest, kind, caring, and respectful, regardless of how they are towards you. Even if your siblings are mean to you, if you persist with your high standards of behaviour they will eventually acknowledge you for it.

You can also choose how to be with your parents. You can choose to play dishonest games with them, having the kind of attitude that it is okay to do something wrong if you think you can get away with it. You might twist stories to make you look good, to inflate your school results, or you might become determined to do wrong things as soon as you are away from parental supervision. This is your choice, but remember each time you make a poor choice, you make it harder for yourself in the long-term. Their love for you might be unwavering, but remember, respect is easily lost and not so easily regained.

Creating conflict is another game where kids set up their parents so that they start to argue, then sit back quietly as it unfolds. The purpose is to get away with things while they are busy arguing, or to get their own way. Passive-aggressive behaviour is another popular game that is extremely manipulative. It is so easy to pretend you don't care, or refuse passively to do things because you really just want to dig your heels in and be the boss. It is usually about showing that you can make your own decisions, that you don't need parents to tell you what to do. The trouble with this game is that you might win in the short-term, but you always lose out in the long-term because the people who are the targets of this behaviour will just want to draw away from you and have as little to do with you as possible. You make it too hard for them if you refuse to cooperate and be part of the team. They give up, lose respect for you. You will lose respect for yourself or feel unloved because they move away from you emotionally. It is an immature, self-destructive behaviour.

You might feel like you are the inventor of these games because you naturally discovered them, but they have been around a long time and they only serve to diminish the quality of family life for all members of the family. By continuing these games beyond the point where they're funny, you will do yourself a disservice because family team activities will be deemed too hard because no one wants to deal with conflict. If you have the kind of mindset that you like to get back at people when they do you wrong, I am asking you to think more deeply about the wisdom of doing that.

When it comes to parents, it is really important to understand that when you are a small child, you expect everything to come from your parent. Your total care is in their hands. As you grow to become an adult, you gradually become their equal in terms of having the power to determine your own destiny. Despite this habit of growing up and expecting your parent to be there for you 24/7, as an adult you will hopefully come to realise that the parent-child relationship is a two-way street. Without give and take, you will find your relationship diminishes.

I have come across 30-year olds who use the most despicable emotional blackmail on their parents, e.g. 'If you really loved me you would share some of your super with me because I really need it.' I know a single, vulnerable parent in her 80s whose daughter has decided she needs her mother's house more than her mother. She has turfed her out into a lesser dwelling against her mother's wishes. This is not only bullying behaviour, but also elder abuse. Self-respect demands that you treat others as you would have them treat you.

Your parents will probably be ever-loving. You may have ill feeling towards them, but you also need to understand that people often set out with little knowledge about how to be a good parent. They do the best they can with what they know at the time. Most would acknowledge that their parenting was less than perfect.

- You can choose how you want to be with your siblings.
- You can choose how you want to be with your parents.

4.6. Negativity and attitude

If you have been told that you have a poor attitude, you will most likely feel very annoyed. Attitude is what is seen on the outside – how others experience you. It is not necessarily how you feel on the inside. You can choose to shrug off complaints about your attitude, though everything is likely to get worse. A crummy attitude will push people away from you. People don't want to help, assist, or work with someone who has a bad or negative attitude.

Attitude is reflected in your body language, your eye contact, and sometimes in what you don't say as much as what you do say. Think about an employment situation where you really want the job and the money that comes with the work. If you are asked to do something in a particular way and you follow the instructions, but at the same time you shrug your shoulders and screw up your face, your body language is likely to indicate that you don't care. It might be that you feel scared because you don't know what you are doing, but this is not what will show on the outside. Don't fool yourself by thinking that others cannot read your body language. Monitor how you might look to others.

An attitude of entitlement is misplaced. We each have many rights under Australia's civil and criminal laws and, while social services provide some guarantee of an ability to fund some basics of our existence, there is no entitlement beyond that. If you think you are entitled to a good job, good income, holidays, and more, then you will have to think again. The world owes you nothing. You will have to work hard for anything you want.

If you are feeling down or negative about the world, it is easy to project this kind of attitude onto everyone and everything around you. In this case you are choosing to look through a negative lens. It is easy to blame the crappy things going on in the world for causing your negative attitude, because that means you can sit back and refrain from doing anything constructive. On the other hand, if you choose to look at life through a positive lens, you will find that good things happen. You will see opportunities and be open to them. Experiment with both these attitudes and notice the differences in yourself and those around you. As human beings, we rarely see reality because we always look through the lens of our own experience so you do have a choice.

It takes courage and bravery to let go of negativity, because negativity can be both seductive and comfortable. It allows you to never be disappointed. This is a cute game. If you are negative about your achievements then you have an excuse not to bother. The trouble is, in maintaining this attitude, you are hurting yourself. They stunt your emotional growth and limit your life.

Negativity takes many forms. You might put yourself down. You might have such a strong need to be perfect that anything less is a disaster. You might have a strong desire for approval. A defeatist stance of, 'I can't be bothered' also comes out of a negative attitude, as does an intolerance of others.

By contrast, if you are emotionally resilient you will block those negative thoughts and tell yourself how you want to be. You can choose to have a can-do attitude; to understand that there are some things you have to do for the ultimate reward of future success. If you are emotionally resilient you will look for the good in others and accept failure as an opportunity for growth. It is about having a positive attitude to learning and personal development. An emotionally resilient pathway is by far a happier journey. Try it! Move through, move on, and be open to new experiences. It will be fun.

It's important to know how you really feel. If you are feeling hurt or left out, it is easy to project an attitude that says something different in order to cover up how you feel. This cover-up attitude may not be in your best interests because the person you usually hurt the most is yourself. Others respond to you according to what they see from the outside.

If you present as thankful and grateful for things people do for you, they are likely to continue to help and support you. If you present as grudging, negative, or ungrateful, the person involved will see no point in continuing to try and assist you. There is a very old poem: 'Laugh and the world laughs with you, weep and you weep alone.' (Wilcox, 1883) Try to stop feeling sorry for yourself. Take time out and take stock of how much fun you are missing out on through your negativity. Is this what you really want?

Look for your future in areas that hold your passion. You might wish to set yourself some goals, but remember, it is the journey that counts. There is no point in struggling all your life for a goal that, once achieved, begins to feel empty. Be open to redirecting your energies in areas that intrigue and draw you. Remember, who you spend your time with will likely determine your future. If you work hard to achieve the small tasks, you will develop all kinds of expertise. One success leads to another. If you are open to the opportunities available to you and have a sense of gratitude with each new experience, your journey will be meaningful and fulfilling, and your end goal will be infinite because you will continue to grow and learn. Be positive!

- It takes courage to let go of negativity because negativity can be seductive and comfortable.
- Look for your future in areas you have passion.
- Who you spend your time with will likely determine your dreams and goals.

Chapter 5

5

Emotions

5.1. *Building and valuing your self-esteem*

5.2. *Resilience: growing and learning from mistakes*

5.3. *Overcoming loneliness*

5.4. *Sexuality*

5.5. *Falling in love*

5.6. *Understanding grief*

5.7. *When everything seems hopeless*

5.8. *Overcoming stress, overthinking, and anxiety*

5.9. *Self-harming behaviours*

5.10. *Controlling your anger*

5.11. *Resilience and leadership*

5.1. Building and valuing your self-esteem

Have you ever thought, *I wish I was taller*, or, *I wish I was more attractive*? It is normal to have these kinds of fleeting thoughts, but it is not healthy to fixate on them. It is so easy to get sucked into image concerns, especially when there are so many media stories around with models who have spent thousands creating their image with surgery and special effects. Always remember that every human being has their own charm. This shines through most when we are happy.

It is so important to keep your self-esteem healthy. When you have choices to make, set some goals that you know you can achieve that, when accomplished, will make you feel good about yourself. Observe how your self-esteem grows and gives you confidence. Watch your own self-talk. If you are constantly putting yourself down you are simply assaulting your own self-esteem. This reduces your resilience. Resilience is the ability to pick yourself up when something goes wrong, being determined to push ahead, always believing in yourself. If you defeat yourself through constant negative self-talk, a downward spiral in your self-esteem is inevitable.

What do you think would happen if a soccer coach gathered the players before the grand final and told them that they are a bunch of idiots with pathetic skills? They are certainly not likely to go out and win the final. Professional sporting clubs pay a fortune for hypnotherapists to teach players to talk positively to themselves. You need to become your own coach. Whenever a negative thought creeps in, push it aside with a phrase that means something to you, e.g. 'I have got this' or, 'I can do it'.

Do yourself a favour: appreciate yourself as a unique and loved being. There is only one of you, and you hold a treasure chest of personality features. If you are a good person who is kind and caring to others, you will be much loved. What's more, one day you will find someone who values those features. Be kind to yourself. Remember that if you feel good about yourself you will go on to achieve bigger and better personal goals, whatever you choose them to be.

Comparing yourself to others
One of the most important things you will ever learn in your life is that there is no value in comparing yourself to others. The harder you look, the more you will see other people who

seem better than you in some way. It is crucial that you learn that this pathway not only leads to discontent, it is also quite inaccurate. Let me explain.

As human beings, we see only what we want to see. The more you focus on something, the more you are likely to notice it. If you look at a gorgeous garden bed and focus only on the one dead flower, you will miss the opportunity of seeing all the living flowers. Everyone has something that is especially appealing to others. For example, when someone smiles, that is the thing that takes our attention – that is what we look at. We don't focus on the one pimple on an otherwise healthy and beautiful face.

Another way to think about this is with movies. We so easily pick out the bad guy in movies. When someone is mean, selfish, or up themselves, that is what we see instantly. It has nothing to do with body shape or size. When someone is smiling, relaxed, and happy with themselves, this is what we see.

If you are still feeling self-conscious or low, you can always improve your physical appearance by being fit and healthy, and taking some personal pride in your appearance. If you are overweight, then exercise and eat well. There is a whole media world intent on making you feel inadequate so that you will buy their products. Don't get sucked in. If you eat healthily on a daily basis, small portions of the not so good foods will not be a problem to you.

Enjoying food should be done with deliberate and conscious joy. Eat slowly, enjoy the aroma, texture, and taste of food. It is a well-known fact that if you eat with awareness, the more you eat of one particular food, the less pleasurable it becomes as you continue to eat it. There is a diminishing pleasure with increased quantity. Try eating small amounts of the occasional foods, and thoroughly enjoy it. You will find that after one or two mouthfuls, it will become less attractive to your palate. You don't have to eat it all, just enough to enjoy the taste. Stick to healthy daily food, but make sure you allow yourself some fun with food, too.

Revel in a healthy lifestyle with lots of activity. Look around you. People are all built differently. There are so many shapes and sizes. You will be attractive if you are living a healthy lifestyle, are happy, and have lots of ways to feel good about yourself. Someone wise will come along and love you just as you are. This is so much healthier than attracting someone who is seeking the trophy partner to look good by their side. The qualities that sustain long-term relationships are honesty, respect, kindness, thoughtfulness, responsibility, and the ability to work hard in a team effort. Stunning good looks do not figure in that list at all.

- Consciously make choices that build your self-esteem.
- There is no value in comparing yourself to others.
- If you are hurting from criticism, check that it is coming from someone you respect and admire.

5.2. Resilience: growing and learning from mistakes

If you are so afraid of making a mistake that you recoil from anything that is new, then you are missing out on life. If you do take risks and venture out of your comfort zone you are bound to make a mistake at some stage. The phrase 'human error' acknowledges that all humans make mistakes sometimes. Organisations put lots of checking systems in place to pick up quickly on human error.

For instance, maybe you know someone who has been caught stealing. This does not necessarily make this person a bad person. If they say, 'Yes, I stuffed up, I won't do it again' then all is well. The mistake will be forgiven by all. If, on the other hand, your friend says, 'Who cares?' and keeps stealing, then your friend will become known as someone who disregards other people's property, and is therefore a not very nice person.

Everyone makes mistakes and does silly things as they grow up. Even grown adults make mistakes. The important thing is that you learn from your mistakes, own up, and take responsibility for them, as well as make reparations to those who have been hurt by your actions. Don't forget to care for yourself. Be tough on yourself in taking responsibility for your actions, but be kind to yourself. Celebrate that you took a risk rather than destroy your self-esteem because of one mistake.

No matter what, remember that you are still a good person, unless you deliberately set out to do evil or cause harm to others. You have probably been told this many times, but it does not only apply to mistakes. It also applies to various life crises that can come along. It is important to remember that it is not the crisis that counts, but how you handle it that will impact the rest of your life. If you have inadvertently or deliberately contributed to a crisis in your family, then apologise and try to fix things up. Your family will still love you, even though they may not like what you have done, or not done.

When you do something wrong, it is important to understand what the need was that drove your behaviour. Was it peer pressure and wanting to be liked? Was it a shortage of money? Was it a way to bring attention to yourself? Was it just a spontaneous, silly thought that you acted on? Have you been feeling unhappy lately? Did you forget to think about consequences? Find a better way to fulfil the need that drove your behaviour, and be alert should the same situation arise in the future.

At times, you may feel you have let your family down. Maybe you have. It is that trust wall again! Maybe it has been shattered, and now you have to rebuild it brick by brick. This might be painful, and your parents will probably put restrictions on you until they feel they can trust you again. You will have a lot of convincing to do to show them that you have learnt from your mistake.

Remember, one brick at a time and they will regain their trust in you. It will all be good again before you know it, as long as you make sure you don't give them any further cause to distrust you. Be patient! Remember, it really is not clever to make the same mistake twice.

- You can break someone's trust in less than a minute.
- Rebuilding trust will take much longer.

5.3. Overcoming loneliness

Some people live in their head and avoid accessing their emotions. Other people are strongly connected to their emotions and are very sensitive to the world around them. They take close notice of things other people say, and feel easily hurt by criticism. They often fear upsetting other people. While there is nothing wrong with having strong emotions, it can feel quite lonely if you have no way of expressing what you feel. If those around you shy away from talking about their emotions it can feel like you are the only one who feels things deeply. This can lead to feelings of loneliness. If you are a sensitive person it is important to choose friends who are not afraid to express their feelings.

Friendship groups will often talk about everything but their emotions. When you are brave enough to open up to one of your friends or family members to let them know that you are feeling down, sad, or lonely, you might be surprised at the way they respond. Rather than isolate yourself by thinking you are alone with your deep feelings, be brave and reach out to others. It will make the world of difference to you.

It is natural to feel lonely in lots of situations, and it is not something to panic about – it will pass. There is nothing wrong with keeping to yourself, as long as you are happy to do this. This is expected when going into a new class or starting a new school. This is a time when you need to be patient. Understand that it takes a couple of weeks to get to know people whenever you join a new group. It is far more important to make the right friends than rush too quickly to make friends with the first people you meet. It is so tempting to fill the gap quickly, rather than take time to decide how that gap would be best filled.

When you have had a great time with friends who then leave, it is natural to have a sense of a lonely gap. You genuinely miss their company. This is a good loneliness because it helps you appreciate the good times. It also gives you a chance to look forward to the time you meet again.

You can also feel lonely when other people are mean or exclude you in a cruel or nasty way. Hopefully this will only be a temporary feeling because you will realise that anyone who treats you like that is really not worth bothering about. If this is happening to you, it is time to look around for new friends who are more mature and respectful.

If you frequently feel overwhelmed by your emotion, it might simply be that you are a naturally sensitive person who feels things very deeply. It can be pretty tough dealing with criticism from other people who try to make out that there is something wrong with you. Being emotionally sensitive can be really lonely until you find someone who is as equally emotionally sensitive as you. Emotionally sensitive people often form strong and lasting relationships. They often hide away, and it is easy to get the impression that most of the world is extraverted and somewhat less sensitive. Rest assured; sensitive people are out there.

Much therapy is done with adults who have difficulty accessing their emotions. Without emotional connections, relationships easily fall into conflict, and often fail. If you are highly sensitive there will be many benefits that come your way. Emotional sensitivity is a wonderful gift if you are able to feel deeply.

The world would be a much healthier place if there were more people who were emotionally sensitive.

Trust that you are okay, that it is far healthier to be able to both think and feel than to be merely living in cognitive thought. This said, when you feel things very deeply but have no one to talk to, loneliness can be a real danger. In these situations, it is really important to try to let your feelings out. If you don't have anyone you can talk to, you could start journaling, writing songs, or talking to someone who will hold your confidentiality.

Humans are all similar. It is so lonely to hold on to your emotions believing that no one else will understand. In reality, many people feel like this. Others would understand you if you trusted them enough to let them know how you feel. Once you have expressed what is troubling you, the loneliness will shift. Your feelings will move to another emotional place and you will experience something different. You will move through the awful feelings to ones that are much more comfortable.

Feelings are more precious than gold. Own them, because they are valuable to you. You can only offer your feelings – they can't be taken away from you – and, if you share your feelings, then you give direct communication from your heart. Feelings may not necessarily be appropriate, politically correct, logical, or rational. They are what they are. They are real.

Try not to be afraid of the strength of your feelings. Only by hanging onto unexpressed feelings do you freeze them in time and become overwhelmed by them. Sharing them will help you feel better. It will also build intimate connections, and you will be well rewarded with close connections.

There is a deeper loneliness that a lot of people feel until they meet a mate who will be theirs for life. Finding the right person takes time, so accept that this kind of loneliness will be there for a while. It is perfectly normal to have this kind of yearning. It is normal and natural. It doesn't need to lead you into depression.

Whatever the kind of loneliness you feel, it is important to work out what the cause is. Doing this can change your situation. Are you stopping yourself from going to new activities? Are you being negative about how others will see you? Whatever it is that is causing your loneliness, be patient. Sometimes it takes time to change things.

If you are feeling lonely for friends, try to look for one or two people who you like and admire. Strike up some common interest that you share; look for opportunities to be with them during activities. Focus on making their life happier or better by saying encouraging things to them. Be interested in them, but know when to back off, and wait for them to show interest in you. Having one or two good friends may make you happier than having heaps of friends you don't know that well.

If you are drawing back from being involved in school activities, you may be doing yourself a disservice. Volunteer for committees, leadership opportunities, or community service. Put yourself out of your comfort zone and try new things with new groups of people. Even if you stuff up, laugh at yourself and others will laugh with you. 'Spreading your wings' is a lovely old expression; it conjures a bird in full flight. When you spread your wings to try new things and make new friends, you will become more *you*.

Trying new things is a good idea for many reasons. One day you might wish to apply for a job. On your resume, it is good to show a range of interests and a history of personal development. This can be shown either through your involvement in the school curriculum or in groups outside of school. Put yourself out there and follow your own interests. You will soon find someone like-minded whom you can befriend. Who knows what you will want in a few years' time? For now, have a growth mindset and see everything as an opportunity to learn, grow, and develop into an adult.

> - When your emotions feel 'locked up', try letting them out little by little.

5.4. Sexuality

Sexuality is as much a part of our humanity as eating and drinking. Our species only exists because of sexual drive and procreation. At the most basic biological level, humans depend on sexuality as a driving force behind many and varied pursuits. Sexuality fuels creative expression, passion for life, and a way of connecting intimately with other human beings.

Wanting to explore your sexuality is perfectly natural. Putting pressure on yourself to understand it all now is not helpful. If you let a relationship unfold you can enjoy the intimate emotional connection that often comes with physical attraction. There is so much to learn and manage about the social and emotional dynamics in a relationship without jumping too quickly to full sexual intimacy. There is also a great deal at stake. Once you engage in sexual intercourse you enter the realms of adult responsibility where you need to protect yourself against pregnancy. No matter how good the protection is, you could still be forced to deal it, not to mention regular medical check-ups for STIs.

These are tough things to deal with, and the emotional impact can sometimes last a lifetime. Guys need to consider the stress it puts on any young girl before they even think of exerting pressure to have sex. My stomach turns when I hear of guys threatening to end a relationship unless they have sex. While this is the sort of guy that girls are better off without, it is also sad when young girls present either with their hearts broken or in total confusion about what to do. Sexual intimacy needs to be part of a relationship. A decision to have full sexual intercourse has to be talked about in advance. In a strong, long-term relationship, there will hopefully be trust and confidence that your partner will be there to support you in any situation that eventuates. By long-term I am not talking a couple of weeks or months, I am talking many months. It is never something that should be rushed into. To do so is immature and foolish. The time will come when you are confident that full sexual intimacy feels right for you.

Most adults will acknowledge that they had a tough time during their teenage years. Understanding your own sexuality can be very confusing. Labels are usually unhelpful and restricting. People can identify as: lesbian, gay, homosexual, heterosexual, bisexual, transgender, a-gender, zie/ze, pansexual, intersex, and more. It is not surprising that the whole area might be confusing.

Sex, sexual orientation, and gender

At birth, our sex is usually reported before anything else, i.e. 'It's a girl!' or, 'It's a boy!' Sex refers to the biology of the genitals and the chromosomes – XX for girls, and XY for boys. Sexual orientation refers to an attraction for the same or opposite sex. For example, heterosexual people are attracted to the opposite sex, gay and lesbian people are attracted to the same sex, and bisexual people are attracted to both. Gender is something different altogether; it refers to how you might be expected to act as your sex (a girl or a boy). Note that stereotypes and expectations of gender vary between cultures and social times.

Some people are born with genitals that are not easily classified as male or female. Others are born with different responses to hormones, or have a different chromosomal makeup. These people are said to be born intersex. They are a normal variation of nature, but one that has traditionally not been freely spoken about.

Transgender refers to people who commonly experience a different inner sense of their gender to their biology. While some transgender people are happy with their own body, others choose to modify or change their bodies to bring them into line with their internal sense of themselves. There is the same range or sexual orientations as the rest of the population within the transgender community. Pansexual and a-gender people reflect a reluctance to identify as either male or female sex or gender.

With all this, it is not surprising that you may ask, 'What am I?' What is important is that you are comfortable with your own sexuality, however that unfolds. Hold back from any kind of labelling that defines and restricts your sense of yourself; hold back on plans to change your body. It is much more important to be comfortable with yourself mentally, emotionally, and spiritually – it is better to just *be* and to enjoy *being*.

You need not feel troubled if you feel differently from those around you, and you do not need to feel alone. Many people question their gender at some stage, though few freely admit it because they are worried about judgement. If you are not comfortable speaking to those close to you, then seek out a mental health professional. They deal with these kinds of issues all the time.

Sex drive
Human beings are gifted with sexual drive. It gives us great strength and motivates us to procreate in order to secure the existence of the human species. Know that masturbation is a natural way to satisfy this drive when you do not have a sexual partner. It is a good way to release tension, and is a natural part of healthy sexuality. The only thing to watch out for here is that emotional distress of any kind can lead to excessive masturbation used as an emotional escape. This is a cue that you might need to talk to someone about all the issues that are worrying you. Remember, we are all ordinary people who have ordinary problems.

Shared sexual intimacy when based on trust and sound relationship will be honest, relaxed, and fun. A good relationship is one in which you have time together and time apart, where you enjoy coming together for companionship, cuddles, affection, and intimacy as the relationship progresses. There has to be compromise between one's own wants and the wants of the other. It is joyful to share worlds with another, always having high regard for the welfare and best interests of the other.

Casual sex, on the other hand, rarely proceeds to become a long-term relationship. 'Friends with benefits' (sex with no relationship ties beyond friendship) may ultimately hurt someone else, and lead to feelings of shame and guilt. Think carefully about what you are doing and look after the emotional health of both parties.

Leading someone on means pretending you really like a person just so you can have sex. It is cruel and abusive to have sex with someone because you are being pressured by your mates or your girlfriends. Sexual intimacy is not a trophy, or a rite of passage; it is an important part of an emotionally intimate relationship. Anyone who ridicules you because you have not had intercourse is extremely immature, and not someone you should take notice of.

There is a variety of pornography visible in social media, and while people often laugh about it, there is a serious side to consider. There is no getting away from the fact that pornography is skilfully constructed by people with less than honourable motives. There are developers who relish the money made from sales and advertisements, and there are those who entice unwary individuals into sexual activity with the intention of exploitation. Pornography is also often demeaning in the way that it portrays individuals as sex objects. The making of pornographic videos has usually involved vulnerable young people being exploited.

Pornography takes the emotion out of sexual behaviour, and is likely to seduce you into dangerous and unhappy territory. What you watch will likely become the norm for you. If you are not careful to distinguish between fantasy and genuine relationship-building that comes with respectful love-making, you will be in danger of tainting or diminishing otherwise beautiful emotional intimacy. Growing up is about is about learning to control your own behaviour and refraining from the temptations that can lead you down the unhelpful pathways that demean the healthy ways of living. Set your own standards of behaviour, and stand by others who are too weak or vulnerable to resist coercion.

Boundaries and protection

If you and your friend wish to take your relationship into sexual intimacy, this has to be talked about openly between the two of you. No means no, in any circumstance. It is not as simple as just listening out for a 'no'. It is critical that verbal consent is gained before any intimate touching happens. Know that when you engage in sexual intimacy you hold the other person's emotional wellbeing in your hands. It is so important to be honest and open about your feelings. Be clear and talk to each other about how far into intimacy you wish to go before you both get into the moment. Be content with close and intimate friendship without feeling pressure to have sex because that is what other kids talk about.

Young women say they have sex to keep their boyfriend, or so they won't be talked about if they don't oblige. Young men say they want the girl to prove their love or they want to have sex in order to own the girl. This is all immature thinking. It is so wrong! Girls are not possessions and should never be blackmailed into having sex for any reason. Similarly, boys are not sexual objects expected to perform when required. Sexual intimacy has to have mutual consent and mutual protection, mutual responsibility and mutual confidentiality.

You need to respect the right of the other person to control the amount of sexual intimacy that happens. To go beyond that is disrespectful. If you ignore the 'no' then you are committing a criminal offence – you are no longer in a consensual relationship, and this is sexual assault. Note that in some states like Tasmania it is against the law to have sex with anyone who is asleep, unconscious, or passed out.

It is important always to act in keeping with your moral conscience. This is an accumulation of all the things you have learnt about right and wrong as you have grown up. When you move outside the bounds of your moral conscience you are struck with a feeling of shame. For instance, posting intimate photos of your partner on the internet would be a despicable act resulting in considerable hurt, embarrassment, and shame for both you and your partner. Outside the bounds of your moral conscience you will also lose the respect of those around you and, more importantly, your own self-respect.

If you feel you have to talk to other people about your intimacies, then you are not mature enough to engage in sexual intimacy. Sexual intimacy is very personal and private in nature. Gossip is quickly passed on and can result in extreme hurt and personal devastation. If you breach the privacy of others there may also be legal ramifications. Be respectful and keep knowledge of shared sexual behaviour between you and your partner. Stand up for respectful behaviour and do not engage in sexual slagging just because those around you have arrogant or disrespectful attitudes to the opposite sex. Mental, physical or sexual abuse of any kind changes lives. It can result in trauma that can torment someone for a whole lifetime.

Brushing bad behaviour off and ignoring it is sometimes more shameful than the initial bad behaviour. If you make a mistake, this is where you own up and face the consequences. You then try to restore the harm you have caused as much as you can. You try to make things right again. When you have done all this then, at some point it is important to forgive yourself with the undertaking that you will never repeat the behaviour.

As mentioned previously, sexual intimacy should only happen when neither party feels pressured; when the relationship is at a stage that it can handle adult responsibilities like sexual health testing, unplanned pregnancy, and emotional commitment.

Contraception is changing all the time. At the time of writing, the most common methods of contraception are condoms, the contraceptive pill, Implanon, and Depo Provera injections. More permanent methods of contraception include vaginal intrauterine devices, and there are also emergency contraception pills that, depending on the type, can be taken up to 72 hours after intercourse (it is best to take this straight away, and double-check the timeframe with your pharmacist).

Remember, pregnancy protection is one thing, but you also need protection from STIs (Sexually Transmitted Infections). Condoms and gels are commonly used for this purpose, though gels only target sperm, so are not the safest option. Protecting yourself is important. You can learn about how to take adequate protection by talking to a sexual health nurse, doctor, or a parent if you are unsure.

Girls carry a huge burden of responsibility when it comes to sex. The risk of pregnancy is real. The burden of STI contraction means the necessity for sexual health checks. For a girl, having sex means moving very quickly into the adult world of responsibility, and is something that should have some security attached to the responsibility. Any guy who blows aside these considerations and puts pressure on his girlfriend is just plain selfish and only interested in his own physical needs. Remember, even if consent is given and the nature of the sexual intimacy that follows is not according to your wishes, you still have the right to say no. No means no at any point of a sexual encounter.

If premarital sex is against your religious beliefs or the morality you have been brought up with, then understand that even in marriage sex and love should go together, though sometimes this is not reality. Sex should be an expression of love, but it is not love itself, and should not be passed off as such. Love is about caring and kindness for another, and this should flow over into the sexual act. Forced sexual intercourse, even within marriage, is rape.

From another perspective, some young women express a powerful drive to have a baby in order to make their world meaningful. The say that they can't wait to have someone to love, someone who will love them as a mother. It is as if they are so untrusting of the world to provide for them that they become determined to make their own little family. After becoming pregnant they often express feeling totally overwhelmed by the responsibility of having a young baby to care for 24-hours a day on their own. The romantic notion of being a mum has hidden realities that hurt. Being a mum is the toughest role ever.

When a young women deliberately tricks a guy into impregnating her, it could be for the above reasons, but sometimes it comes from a desperation to keep their guy in a long-term relationship. This is immature behaviour. It denies the impact that a pregnancy has on a young man who is suddenly thrust into the adult world of parenting without his consent. It is a thoughtless, cruel, and despicable thing to do, regardless of whether the mother wants him to have access to the baby that results.

Remember, good sex is safe, pleasurable, wanted, enjoyed, and consented to by both parties with full consideration of the responsibilities involved. It is wrapped in mutual respect, trust, upfront communication, and respectful boundaries.

Intimacy and attraction
Whether you are attracted to people of the same or opposite sex, sexual intimacy is something you don't have to rush into immediately. If you are confused about whether your sex is different from the gender identity you were born with, just take your time and trust that you will evolve in a way that fits for you. The main thing is that you choose good and honourable people to be with.

Attraction for others comes in many forms, and for many reasons. As you come to understand yourself, your experience of life and relationships will lead you on your own journey. Refrain from being caught into stereotypes and labels. Labels are not helpful. They bring connotations of choice about a way of living and then seem to confine the way you view your sexuality. You are a unique and valuable individual. You do not have to fit a label. Be whoever you want to be. You have a right to be accepted and to be treated with respect.

Teenagers often experience feelings of attraction to friends of the same sex. This is all part of getting to know and understand your own sexuality. It takes a little time before you become comfortable with that part of your life. It is not necessary to jump to any conclusions about your sexuality just because you feel attracted to someone.

Be wary of criticism. When individuals protest loudly about same-sex attraction, they are often neurotically worried about their own sexuality. If you have to tell family and close friends about your sexuality being different to what they expect, it can be very scary. Your family may need time to adjust and time to think through their own values. You are who you are, and your family will love you whatever choice you make. How your family reacts in the short-term is not necessarily an indication of how they will be in the long-term.

If there is any rejection, know that it says more about the person and their ignorance than about you. At the end of the day, beauty is beauty wherever you see it. A beautiful human being is one who is kind and caring of others. Look after yourself! If you feel different, or if you are worried about your sexual identity, go and talk to someone you trust. It can be very scary to experience any kind of discrimination, or to feel pressured to be something you are not. Don't bottle it up. Talking to someone reliable will really help.

Sexuality and emotions
Just as an emotional connection can bring both happiness and hurt, so can sexuality. It can fuel kindness and love, and it can also fuel hatred and abuse. It can be a gentle expression of love, affection, and caring, or it can be used at the expense of another for self-gratification, exploiting, and demeaning another.

Sexuality that is paired with love, respect, and kindness is beautiful and uplifting. Sexuality paired with self-gratification at the expense of another is degrading for both perpetrator and the target of the behaviour. One of the lowest deeds any human can engage in is to use physical force or emotional manipulation for the purposes of sexual self-gratification.

Sexual urges are nothing to be ashamed of. Managing those urges in a way that is respectful of others is what will define you as a decent human being. Trust must be built slowly and surely because sexual intimacy catapults you into adult responsibility. With all forms of sexual intimacy, sexual activity must be consensual. That means that both parties agree all the way, and both parties feel comfortable, safe, and supported.

The important thing is that you choose to be with people who are honourable, trustworthy, and loving, regardless of their sexuality. Whoever you are with should make you feel good about yourself, and encourage you to be who you want to be. They should not try to control who you mix with, or what you spend money on. Remember, too, negative judgements are usually born out of ignorance. Trust yourself, wherever that takes you, and ignore negative judgement. Be courageous about being yourself.

Talk it out
When a relationship feels one-sided, be open and express your feelings. Talk about what you think, feel, and prefer to happen. If the other person is not interested in compromising or moving toward your preferences, then you have to ask yourself, 'Is this really a relationship, or am I just meeting the other person's needs most of the time?' Talk, take time apart, and reflect on what is happening in the relationship. You do not deserve to be used for someone else's ego trip, sexual need, or emotional manipulation. If you are feeling controlled, talk to someone else. Get another perspective.

If you are feeling overly controlled by your friend you need to communicate and explain how you feel. If your friend is intimidating or abusive and it is too hard or unsafe to talk, write them a letter or an email. If you decide to talk to them directly, make sure you have someone with you. Avoid using text if it is safe to get your message to the person in any other way. If the relationship is really intimidating, you may want to express your wish to be left alone. The law will support anyone from being harassed or stalked. Once you have a relationship that has both give and take, the relationship will feel comfortable, easy, and stress-free. If a relationship feels full of drama and trauma then it may be time to acknowledge that this is not the relationship for you.

Ending a relationship
Under normal circumstances, where there is nothing abusive, and you wish to end the relationship, do not break up using text or email. This is cruel and insensitive. There is no shame in wanting to finish a relationship. Communicate all the great times you have had together. Be honest and explain what has gone wrong or what has changed. Be kind and caring, and validate the person you have been spending your time with.

Maybe you are the one who has changed. Maybe you feel you have different interests, maybe you are unsure why, but feel you just need some space for yourself, to concentrate on your interests. Be open and own what you say rather than blame the other person. Know that people often have many relationships 'til they find the one that becomes special for them. If you and your friend have drifted apart, it might simply mean that there has been insufficient meshing of all the things that contribute to relationships, e.g. interests, taste in music, lifestyle, goals, habits, interest in socialising, beliefs, and upbringing. The list is endless.

Text messages are great for facts and making meetup arrangements, but they do not portray emotion. When used to express feelings, texting inevitably misleads or confuses the situation. Texts are so easily misinterpreted and cause so many hurtful disasters in relationships. It is a spineless way to break up. Have the courage to talk to your partner.

If you are on the receiving end of someone breaking up with you, try to be philosophical about it. Losing a relationship is never the end of the world. From each relationship, you will learn more about who you are and what you want in a future relationship. Just because a relationship breaks up, it does not mean that you are to blame, or you are the problem. The capacity for love is a gift. The opportunity of having experienced a sense of loving another is a compounding and enriching experience that is never wasted.

Whether it is your idea or the other person's, any breakup can be tough to deal with because you also have to deal with the grief of losing what you had. Remember that you won't remain in grief even though you might need to feel sad for a time before you move to a happier emotional place. It might help to forgive rather than carry anger. Sometimes it just takes time to recover. This is just a hiccup in life, a natural flow of life's ups and downs.

When you have found what feels like a life partner, the experience of loving them should be relatively easy. Life is too short to be suffering ongoing grief, torment, anguish, or misery. Keep those close who make you feel good about yourself and engender happiness in you. If you are continually made to feel bad about yourself in any way, the relationship may not be the best one for you.

- Growing up is about learning to control your own behaviour and refraining from the temptations that lead you down unhelpful or demeaning pathways.
- It is cruel and abusive to 'lead someone on' emotionally just because you want to have sex.
- It is despicable to trick someone into giving you a baby without their consent.
- Choose to be with people who are honourable, trustworthy and loving.
- Have the courage to talk to your partner if you wish to end the relationship. Never text.

5.5. Falling in love

Falling in love is a wonderful feeling. To have someone special in your life, to be thinking about them all the time, and to miss them when you are apart is very special. Sometimes it can be embarrassing too – you might fumble for words, feel nervous, be too scared to talk, or fear rejection or being regarded as foolish. Facial flushing (blushing) is a dead giveaway. So, if this happens, what do you do?

Firstly, calm down! Human beings have been falling in love since the beginning of time. The intensity of the emotion you feel is not in doubt. You will probably feel quite overwhelmed. Try to be patient. My mother would always say, 'If it is a relationship that is meant to be, then there is plenty of time.' If it is not something special, then patience will allow you to see that before you become too emotionally invested. That saves a lot of hurt down the track. Think about what you want from a relationship – if your friend wants a relationship where you are available every day, and you want a relationship for Saturday night only, then you have a recipe for an early breakup. There are many aspects that determine whether or not a relationship will succeed.

Talk with your special friend and build the relationship on trust. Be open and honest about how you feel. Relationships that are one-sided rarely work unless one party is prepared to be a doormat. Before either invests emotionally in a relationship, there has to be a matching of good communication, values, and expectations. This is hard to do, and even harder when someone is a lot older or younger.

Enjoy the feeling of being in love. At the same time, deep down, be understanding that this special person may not be the one who will meet your every dream. Physical attraction is something that can easily blind us. As you get to know the person, be prepared that you might find out things that make you realise that you have little in common, or maybe you have very different beliefs or values. Remember, liking the person is very different to being attracted to someone. If you are to spend your life with someone, you really need to like them as a person, as well as love and desire them.

Rather than rushing into love, be patient. This allows you to discover each other gradually, over time. If you are working too hard to influence a person into a relationship with you, you are likely to push them away. Relax and take it as it comes. If this relationship doesn't work, it won't be long 'til another will come along.

The idea that you find someone to complete you is fraught with difficulties. It implies that two people merge as one. While it is wonderful if this person grows on you, it is painful and difficult if the attraction diminishes because you have assumed too much. It is far healthier to be strong and independent in your own right and choose to be with someone, rather than need to be with them in order to be complete.

Think about your relationship with yourself. This is the most important relationship you will ever have. Take note of how you feel about yourself, and make sure that your choices are those that make you feel good. Be independent, trust yourself to make good decisions, and, when times are difficult, be your own emotional coach. Celebrate who you are. There is a skill and an art to loving, but when the right person comes along it is easy.

- To spend your life with someone, you need to like and respect them as well as love and desire them.
- Be strong and independent in your own right and choose to be with your special person, rather than 'need' to be with them.

5.6. Understanding grief

Everyone experiences grief at some time in their life. It can be the loss of a pet, a grandparent, or a friend. It can be the loss you feel when you move house, change schools, or even after a relationship breakup. You go through a whole range of emotions when you experience grief. At first there is likely to be a sense of shock or disbelief. Some people react with extreme distress or get really angry. Sometimes people feel quite numb. These sorts of emotions appear in any order and different intensity.

It is also really common to feel some sort of guilt when you lose someone. When someone dies, it never happens at a convenient time when everyone has said what they want to say, or done what they want to do. It is natural to be distressed that you have not done or said the special things you really wanted to say. Grief puts you into a state of confusion as lots of thoughts and feelings come flooding in. Sometimes it is really hard for people to function normally because their grief is so strong.

Tears will help you move through grief. Eventually you will reach a point where you feel you have cried enough. Don't be afraid of being teary; it is wonderfully healthy. If you stop yourself from crying then there is a risk that the grief will build over time and affect you further down the track. Allow yourself to take time out to have a little cry whenever you feel the need. Allow your grief to flow through you. Talk with others, share your memories and your sadness. Celebrate the life of your loved one rather than morn their loss.

Grief can make it hard to sleep, and it can be difficult to think clearly. For some there can be relentless thinking about the loved one, or what has been lost. Clients will express that they feel guilty if they forget their grief for a short time. They seem to have the idea that if they stop thinking about their loved one then they are being disloyal. If you are feeling overwhelmed by grief, it can be helpful in the beginning to allow yourself a special time, say half an hour at the beginning or end of your day to really go into your grief. At this time allow yourself to feel really sad. Have a really good cry. Think about all the happy times and all your fond memories. At the end of that special grieving time, give yourself permission to go on with your life. Know that you can return to your grief at your special time the next day.

As you gradually begin to feel like your old self, you can have your special times a little less frequently. You will gradually move through all the sadness, anger, and hurt. If it is a person you've lost, you will eventually come to a time when you can talk about the person's faults, as well as their strengths, the funny quirks of their personality, and the traits you loved. It will feel comfortable to be even-minded and celebrate the real person, rather than their glorified version.

Everyone grieves differently. Sometimes there is family tension when one person seems to be over it whilst another is still very sad. Sometimes people who barely knew the lost one present as more distressed than close family. These differences are normal and require both tolerance and patience. Just because someone is not shedding tears, it does not mean that their grief is short-lived, or that they are uncaring.

Sometimes your emotional responses can be cumulative. Feelings from the past seem to be added to your current grief. It is possible that you could feel really sad about losing someone you were not close to. It is not unusual for someone to feel extreme anger one minute, then extreme compassion the next. Grief can also be very confusing when there are two opposing feelings experienced at the same time, such as anger and sadness.

Find someone who will help you reassure yourself that you will not feel overwhelmingly sad forever. Grief is a part of living, and we all learn to go on, however, it is important to take a little time out to adjust to loss, and to care for yourself in times of grief. Know that you will eventually move through your grief to a happier place. Don't be afraid of the extreme emotions you feel. They will lessen over time as you learn to accept all the different aspects of the loss.

Take stock of all the positive things and treasured people you currently have in your life. Be grateful for what you have, rather than allow yourself to lament for too long on what you don't. Look beyond yourself and see the beauty around you. Live for the future, not the past.

- Grief is part of living.
- When you lose someone close, celebrate their life.
- Allow yourself time to grieve.
- When you are ready to resume your daily life, take stock of what you have rather than lament for too long on what you have lost.
- With sorrow comes an appreciation of life.

5.7. When everything seems hopeless

It is strange how sometimes all the bad things seem to come together at once. Life happens – sometimes everything is great, and sometimes not so great. You don't have control over all aspects of your existence. When life presents a string of bad things, it is easy to believe everything is hopeless. Try to remember that the very nature of life is that it has ups and downs. Just because you feel down today doesn't mean that you will feel that way forever. Life dishes out good and bad, boredom and excitement, joy and sadness, frustration and exhilaration. Bad times will be replaced by good times. Your task is to just push through the bad times and be patient waiting for the good times.

Be honest with yourself. Stand up and apologise if you have stuffed up. If someone has hurt you, speak out; let them know what you think and feel and, most importantly, how you would prefer to be treated in the future. If the person ignores your requests then they are not the friend you thought they were. You really do not need them.

Families are a bit different. We cannot cast family members aside. If it is someone in your family who keeps hurting you or refuses to listen to you, you may need to seek help from someone else to get through to them that you are really hurting. Don't give up. There is always a way.

To a large degree, you are responsible for your own happiness. You can make your own life happy by staying positive and looking for opportunities to make your life better. No matter what life dishes out there is always something positive that can be gained. I'm not talking about short-term fixes, like drugs; I'm talking about long-term improvements. If you first work out your long-term goals, then the short-term ones will become evident. Life will become easier and much more satisfying.

Ask for help! If you have been really down or depressed for a long time, talk to a doctor. If the doctor fobs you off, then talk to another one. Don't give up until you get some help. A state of depression is something you want to avoid. Depression will lift when you find someone you can talk to with whom you can articulate all the things that hurt, learn how to be more assertive in the future, and feel confident in asking for what you want, rather than caging up all your emotion inside.

Emotional resilience
Having resilience means being able to get up, dust yourself off, and have another go, even though you are hurting. It means persevering and being determined to recover and carry on with whatever you need to do. Being resilient means being flexible and adaptable to changing circumstances. Life is full of ups and downs – some days you will do great things, other days you will stuff up; sometimes you will feel well, sometimes you will feel unwell. In a way, the not so good days make the good days even better.

If you can accept what is, then you can let go of the past and focus on the future. Some things are within our power to change and you can set about doing just that. For the things that aren't, you need the wisdom to be able to accept that you can't change them. This means not beating your head against the wall because it won't help; it will only hurt your head. Then you can set about problem-solving, step-by-step, all the things you can change.

It is natural to want to fill any gap in our lives. You can do this by overworking, making bad friends, taking drugs, or overeating. A gap feels painful, but filling it with the wrong things you can make it even worse. Negativity is something that blocks us from moving on. If you are negative, you will miss the opportunities that come to you. There is always something you can learn from every negative situation, and there are so many life experiences ahead of you that, with a resilient attitude, you can explore and savour.

Avoidance of emotional pain eventually starts to block your resilience. It is not clever. Blocking things out inevitably brings worse pain. The lion that has been caged up will go frantic when finally released. If you feel really upset, allow yourself to have a cry or shed some tears. The best policy is to be honest with yourself and others. Let them know how you are feeling. Be assertive. Yes, even grown men cry – it is healthy. Allowing yourself to feel emotional pain is the healthiest thing you can do because it is something that you will move through. When you do, it makes you stronger.

- Life is full of ups and downs.
- If you allow yourself to express emotional pain, you will move beyond it.
- Only you can choose to be positive rather than negative.
- If you are depressed, find someone you can talk to.
- Accept what is! Know the things you can't change.
- Put your energy into the things you can change.

5.8. Overcoming stress, overthinking, and anxiety

Stress is a driving force – it helps you to get things done on time, to learn your lines for a play, or the rules of the road if you want to get your driver's license. Stress is only a problem when you feel overwhelmed by all you have to do, or when you find yourself in situations that are dampening your spirits. A busy lifestyle with lots of activities and things to remember is both exhilarating and stressful. To sit at home with nothing to do would be less stressful, but probably quite boring. Balance is required.

Understand that it is normal to have anxious thoughts. What you do with them is what determines whether or not you will end up in a state of anxiety. Everyone has this experience at different moments in their lives. It is normal to have anxious thoughts about your first day in a new education setting, a new job, attending a social gathering with a new group of people, travelling overseas, or even walking out the front door. Anxious thoughts are what keep you safe. They stop you from walking straight onto a road where you might get hit by a passing vehicle. They stop you from touching a burning fire. They stop you diving into a relationship that you know will not be good for you.

It is important to find something to do in your life that you really enjoy and do not find stressful. This may be lazing with a good book, watching TV, or having fun with computer games. It is also really important to have a safe zone or place where you can retreat whenever things are rough. Your bedroom may be a safe place where you feel at peace, or perhaps you have a favourite tree to sit under, or a special stuffed toy to curl up with. Even a symbol or picture can be a safe space – anything that reminds you in your heart that you are loved, that you are okay, and that you can get through anything.

You can make your own stress by creating such high expectations for yourself that you have no time to relax, always rushing from one activity to another. Being a perfectionist about everything is a sure road to anxiety. It is an impossible task because life gets complex. If you know you are a perfectionist, try to target your perfectionism. You could do this by playing an instrument, or focusing on particular subjects. Remember, if perfectionism is at the expense of life balance, then sickness or some sort of crisis is likely to occur. If you want to be a true perfectionist then challenge yourself to be a perfectionist in the way you balance the competing elements of your life.

Stress is not something that exists on its own. We make our own stress. What is stressful for one person can be exhilarating for another. It is your perception of stress that determines your personal stress levels. You can be stressed by anticipating all the things that could go wrong, or because someone doesn't like you. You might hold on to bad memories or old hurts, instead of letting them go. You might allow your brain to focus on what ifs rather than be in the moment. Worrying about your health is another way to whip yourself into an anxious state. These kinds of thought patterns will lead you to overthinking everything.

One young client was convinced he had heart problems because he could hear his heart making sounds. All tests revealed that he had a healthy heart. He was so anxious he kept researching heart problems, and became convinced his heart was faulty. When he was busy doing something enjoyable he would forget his anxiety and it went away. This demonstrated that his heart problems were anxiety-induced. If you are worrying about your health, do a quick check to see if you are in serious pain, or have a high temperature. Consult a doctor, or talk to someone close to you first if you are unsure about needing to go to the doctor.

It is commonly believed that people who expect to stay healthy usually do, whereas people who think of themselves as sickly are often sick. If you think that worrying about your health is caused by overthinking and anxiety, breathe in and out slowly. Engage your brain in an activity you enjoy and see how you feel. Does the anxiety go away?

If the stress you are experiencing is severe, then have a think about what it is that is driving your stress. Is it a need to be the best, to be approved of, or to win? Or is it a fear of failure, a fear of losing the respect of others, or being overly critical, especially of yourself? If the stress is uncomfortable then you may need to question your thinking. The stress you are putting on yourself will diminish your actual achievements. In contrast, if you have fun and enjoy what you do, you are more likely to be successful.

Look at your time management and develop some habits that make life easier. Purchase some cheap baskets or trays to help get yourself organised. Have a bag for each activity that you restock, ready for the week. Get work done according to your schedule, assess your sleep habits, and look at how much time you spend on those comfort activities. Read, relax, and try some gentle diaphragmatic breathing. Put your head in a happy heart space by imagining a picture of your favourite, or most happy place. Imagine your happy place as a jigsaw puzzle, where you think about all the individual bits that go together. Examine each part of the picture in detail.

If your sleep routine is not good, make sure you have winddown time without media devices before you sleep. Gradually bring forward the time for bed, but get up at the same time each day. If your sleep regime is totally out of whack and you are sleeping in late then you will need to gradually force yourself to get up a little earlier each day until you get back to a reasonable schedule. Do it gradually, but be persistent.

If you are well-organised and take care of the little things, like having a bottle of water ready in your gym bag, or sitting your music with your instrument, or your hiking gear all in the one spot, your life will be easier to manage. You will be able to give 100% to whatever activity you are involved in. When you have work to do, always start the hard tasks first and work through them one step at a time. The later ones will seem easy to finish. When you have completed each task, take a little time to celebrate your success before you move to the next task.

Sometimes life conspires to bring lots of difficult things all at once. During these times, it is important to live one day at a time and try not to worry too much into the future. There is no point in worrying about things that may never happen. Use some relaxation exercises to calm your body and your mind. Reassure yourself that difficult things are always more manageable after a good night's sleep.

If something is worrying you, do something about it earlier, rather than later. Don't let little things turn into big things because you have left it too long to take action. Allow yourself time to daydream about the things you would like to do in the future. Give space to your daydreams, but don't churn and overthink them.

- Your thoughts are always transient unless you hang onto them and catastrophise them.
- Find something you love doing that allows you to be in the moment.
- Find your safe place for retreat whenever life gets rough.
- Be a perfectionist in the way you balance your life.

Overthinking: you are more than your brain

From the time you were little you were probably told to use your brain; to be sensible, to work it out, to think about consequences, to problem-solve, and to learn. You can be forgiven for thinking that you are your brain, but this is not true. The cognitive part of your brain is great for problem-solving but quite inept when it comes to emotional issues.

Now, emotions also come from the brain, but for the purposes of this discussion I have chosen to regard them as coming from your heart (emotion evolves from a number of areas of the brain, and the exact nature of these connections are not yet fully understood). When the heart is examined under MRI, warm, heartfelt feelings light up the nerve endings around the heart. For therapeutic purposes, the distinction between head and heart is helpful.

The cognitive part of your brain is good for manipulating sensory data (sight, sound, touch, taste, and smell) and making neural connections (pathways) that develop into your thought patterns. The part of your brain that gives you grief with overthinking is a huge network of everything you have ever seen, heard, touched, tasted, or smelt. From the time you are born, the neural connections are made between all your sense data.

This part of your brain is a great little computer to carry around on our shoulders. It takes in sense data and organises it in logical, rational ways. Living in your brain will inevitably lead to stress and anxiety. It is like living in the internet, and never getting out of it. This can overwhelm you because the neural connections are infinite. When you overthink, you ruminate, following the same neural pathways, circling them over and over. When solutions are not obvious, there can be an endless inspection of detail. You think harder. The lack of a solution to a situation that is insolvable, or a situation that is beyond your control causes distress and leads to a state of anxiety because the degree of overthinking is intolerable.

When you stay in your brain and see everything in a rational way, the lack of emotional and spiritual connection erodes your wellbeing. You can't get the green light because there is conflict with what you are feeling in a less conscious way. When you allow yourself to drop into your emotional self, the future pathway often becomes crystal-clear. You suddenly feel what it is you want.

If you want to become a master at managing your anxiety there are a few things you need to understand.

How your brain works

As the blood flows into the brain it causes the neurons to fire whenever a new connection is made. Millions of connections are formed; some become automatic, like learning to walk, or starting a car. Your first efforts are pretty wobbly, but the skill gradually becomes ingrained. A huge number of our behaviours are automatic. With automatic/addictive behaviours like cigarette smoking, the neural pathway is thick and strong. It is so easy to slip down the neural pathway, and yet, for each time you say no to a cigarette, you build a new neural connection that gradually develops into a strong neural pathway. It gets stronger and stronger until, eventually, the old cigarette pathway prunes away through lack of use.

When you are in fight or flight mode, the amygdala clings onto blood as it comes through the brain. Fear can produce a fight/flight type response. In extreme fear, people do silly things because the outer part of the brain where decisions are made does not get sufficient blood flow with the necessary oxygen. Learning how to calm your fear and focus your brain on non-anxious thoughts is important. If you allow yourself to be consumed by anxious thoughts of failing before an exam, your blood flow to your brain will lessen and your cognitive capacity will be reduced. Anxiety up = brain power down!

Understand that your brain never stops. That is normal. The computer was first modelled from the brain. Like the internet, there are infinite connections that can be made in the cognitive part of your brain. Thousands of thoughts are created as new neural connections are made. The neurons fire and the idea passes on to be replaced by another in rapid succession. Have you ever had the experience of having a fantastic idea only to find a second later that it has disappeared? It can be so frustrating when you just can't recall it. The neurons have fired and the thought is gone in a flash.

Just imagine how good it would be if you allowed your anxious thoughts also to pass through your brain in a flash. This will happen once you accept that it is normal to have anxious thoughts and choose to pay no attention to them.

Anxiety happens when you insist on holding onto the anxious thoughts and then exaggerating them: 'Oh no,' and, 'What if...?' or, 'That is awful', and, 'If I am thinking that, it must be real.' When you engage in this kind of catastrophising, anxiety is inevitable. Be aware of what the cognitive part of your head is doing. Let the anxious thoughts go and take control of what your brain is engaged in.

Find a good distraction from overthinking
Tell your brain to do something that is pleasant, fun, or productive. Refuse to engage in anxious overthinking. Sing a song, recite the alphabet backwards, or construct a shopping list. Find something that works for you. It does not matter what the task is, as long as your brain is engaged in the activity. Whenever you start feeling anxious, ask your brain to engage in your special task and notice how the anxiety lifts in the short-term. You can't get anxious if your brain is working on something else.

If you find that you are too engulfed in your thoughts to do anything, look around you and use your five senses to bring you into the here and now. Everything you see, hear, smell, taste, or touch is in the present, the here and now. The here and now brings relief from anxious thoughts that reside in the past or the future.

Adopt a new philosophy
Managing anxious thinking requires a shift from your head to your heart. If you struggle with identifying your feelings, it is worth taking time to try to master this shift from head to heart.

Try to come up with the vision of something that really touches your heart, like the person you love the most. When you access that emotion, note how warm and lovely the feeling is. This is often called a happy space, or a happy heart space. Hold onto that feeling. Savour and enjoy all the feelings that come to the fore. Even if it is too hard to put words to the feelings, note how strong and real those feelings can be. Get used to the idea that your heart space is a warm, comforting place. It is not somewhere you have to run away from. Your emotions are where you find your true directions in life. This is the part of you that helps you choose what you want. This is the part of you that makes life worthwhile.

The power to overcome anxious thinking lies first in being aware of what your brain is doing. Then it is your strength of wanting to do something in a different way that will give you the power to overcome those anxious thoughts. Once you know what you want or how you want to be, it is easy to focus your head in that direction. Think of the athletes going to the Olympics; their extensive daily training over their entire career for what is sometimes a few minutes in competition. As they get closer, their thoughts are flooded with all the things that could go wrong, yet their strength lies in saying, 'Shut up, brain, I'm not going there. I WANT to focus on my training, going to the Olympics, and having a great time. I want to do the best I can.'

The neural connections in your brain are logical and rational. The brain thrives on instructions. If you tell your brain you need to get home it will dutifully tell you which way to turn until you get there. If you tell your brain to focus on, 'What if I fail,' or, 'What if no one likes me,' or, 'I am hopeless,' it will dutifully go down that pathway, and will keep going with more and more what ifs until you say, 'That is enough. I need to stop thinking that way.' If you fail to take charge of your brain you will end up at the end of a really long corridor of fearful thinking where you are depressed or highly anxious. Just like a computer, the cognitive part of your brain will dutifully carry out whatever task you give it.

Remember, you are much more than the cognitive part of your brain. You have an emotional self, a physical self, and a spiritual self. When your head, heart, and body are all working together in the moment, you are in a good spiritual space, the healthiest mental space you can ever be. Some people get this from prayer, some from sailing, or being in the forest. Sporting stars refer to this when they say, 'I was just in my zone.' This zone is in the here and now, in the moment.

Find your special spiritual place and notice how you are anxiety-free whilst there. When anxious thoughts intrude you have the power to choose to make your brain focus in a direction that is anxiety-free and helpful.

Avert panic attacks with deep breathing and refocusing

Allowing yourself to be swallowed up in a reaction of fear will stop you from thinking through your situation in a calm and rational way. When you get anxious you most likely hold yourself in a tense position, caving your shoulders in and breathing in a very shallow way. Your brain goes into panic mode because it starts to lack oxygen. It sends a message to your heart to pump harder. You start to perspire as if you have just finished a run. This is an uncomfortable feeling that sets up more fearful thinking that it won't stop. A feedback loop develops as your brain gets less and less oxygen.

If you find yourself in this situation, force yourself to take in a few really big, deep breaths, and you will find these horrible biological symptoms of a panic attack will wane. If you feel a panic attack coming on, step outside if you can. Look around you and open up your chest and breathe really deeply. Ground yourself in your senses: what can you see, what do you hear, what textures can you feel around you, what can you taste, or smell? This process will bring you into the here and now while the increased oxygen to your brain settles the panic reaction.

While this gives temporary relief, the next step requires that you manage the thinking going on in the cognitive part of your brain. Make your brain focus on something of your choice, something other than the major stressor. Take time out to enjoy whatever it is that helps you feel calm. You might choose to sing your favourite song to yourself, recite the alphabet backwards, or construct your shopping list for the weekend. It does not matter what you choose as long as your brain has to work hard to complete the task. While your brain is working on this task it is not following the previous neural pathway that creates anxiety for you.

When you have really calmed down, follow up by asking yourself what you want in this particular situation. Reassure yourself that you could face even the worst-case scenario. Then try to take a more balanced approach to your situation. Work out what is of the highest priority for you and choose how you want to handle yourself in this situation.

Make the switch from your head to your heart
It is rubbish to believe that you are just an anxious person; that you inherited it from a parent, and are stuck with it for life. What you may have inherited is a way of dealing with the world. If you suffer from anxious thinking, then you have acquired a neural patterning that destroys or demeans you, and probably engulfs you in fear. When the anxiety engulfs you, you will find you are in fantasy of the past or the future, rather than in the present. What you have inherited is a tendency to believe in your head as your authority, your ruler. By contrast, it is your heartfelt feelings that will help you choose the directions you wish to take in life. Once you work out what you want, you have the power to push through any anxious thought that gets in your way.

Work at distinguishing between thought and feeling on a daily basis. Ask yourself six times a day, 'What has been going on in my head?' 'What am I feeling?' 'What is my body telling me?' 'Am I in a good spiritual space, meaning my head, heart, and body are all engaged in something I want to do?'

If the answer is no, then set about getting yourself back into the here and now. Ask yourself what you want and how you want to be in whatever situation is troubling you.

Remember, your thoughts are always fleeting unless you hang onto them, catastrophise them, and bring them into your reality. Just because you have an anxious thought, it doesn't mean that you have to listen to it. That thought is just the result of a neural connection that you have made through habit. You can't remember every single thought you had in the last 10 minutes, because they pass through so quickly. Let the troublesome ones go and create some better ones. Switch from your head to your heart and ask yourself, 'What do I want? How do I want to deal with this?' Trust your heart to overrule your head.

You can then use your head just like a computer to double-check the safety of your chosen journey. As long as you are directing your thoughts you won't be engulfed by them. Start thinking of your head as a computer, a tool that you can use as required rather than one that dominates everything else.

Hearing voices can reflect heightened anxiety
Anxiety and stress are a big part of life – it can be what causes us to get up in the morning, to catch the bus on time, and to get assignments in by the due date. If you learn to use stress to fire you up and get you into action then you won't be caught up in overthinking everything. If you overanalyse and overthink everything you will likely end up feeling anxious, tired, and unmotivated. This is not nice!

It is not unusual to worry about your own mental and emotional health during stressful times. It is common to be scared by the intensity of your feelings, and it is important to understand that heightened anxiety can induce you to hear voices. I have come across young people who feel too ashamed to tell anyone because they fear they are going crazy. With heightened anxiety, hearing a voice or voices can seem convincingly real, and it can very scary. More often than not it is not anything psychotic, but rather a result of heightened anxiety. It is also well-known that some drugs can induce frightening visual pictures in your brain.

This feels different to self-talk which some people are not aware they use. When you are really stressed you can have a heightened awareness of your internal dialogue – you become more focused on it. Self-talk is healthy and very helpful in many situations. Athletes use it to push themselves to higher performance. Try to pay attention to your own self-talk and notice when you use it. Have a short phrase that is meaningful to you. Say it to yourself over and over again in really tough situations when you need to keep your cool and reduce your anxiety. Use your self-talk to reassure you.

It is important to find out what it is that is causing your symptoms. If the voices are prompted by anxious thinking, it is easy to get help. There are anxiety management strategies that you can implement so that your anxiety never reaches those heights again. Be brave! Counsellors and medical practitioners deal with this kind of thing every day. If the symptoms seem more than an anxious focus on your self-talk, then seek help; the earlier the better, as early intervention usually brings a quicker recovery. Most of the population suffer from anxiety at some time in their lives, and your symptoms need to be talked about with a doctor and/or mental health professional as soon as possible.

- You are much more than the cognitive part of your brain. You have an emotional self, a physical self and a spiritual self.
- Thoughts are always fleeting unless you hang onto them, catastrophise them and bring them into your reality.
- It is common to feel scared by intense feelings.
- Heightened anxiety can induce someone to 'hear voices'.

5.9. Self-harming behaviours

There are many kinds of reasons why individuals engage in self-harm. People can sabotage themselves over and over by continuing a behaviour that they know will lead them to trouble, like cheating, stealing, or drug-taking. Cutting or leaving marks on the skin is generally an escape from feeling very low, depressed, or anxious. Clients say that when they feel real physical pain it is better than feeling emotional pain. Sometimes it is a way of feeling a sense of control when everything else is in chaos, or it can even be a tricky game of getting attention. The trouble is that these behaviours have very short-lived results. They actually make life harder than the initial problem.

If you are cutting, it is really important to get some help from a counsellor or someone you trust. The sooner you do this, the better. Running away from emotions does not work. When you start talking to someone, you articulate what it is that hurts. You start to identify what the pain is that you want to escape, and you can start on the strategies to remove the pain altogether.

If it is one of your friends who is self-harming, be very strong with them and explain that unless they are prepared to get some help from a parent or a professional, they are giving you no alternative other than for you to talk to someone on their behalf. Remember that little game mentioned previously, the, 'I want the attention and I am not prepared to help myself' game. It is really hard, but don't get sucked into thinking you must not betray your friend.

Friends who self-harm need something to change in life in order to feel happy. Sitting and talking to you is not going to achieve that. It might be a good start, but your friend needs to take responsibility and accept the need to do something differently if things are going to permanently change. Your friend needs to communicate the situation to a trusted adult.

- Running away from emotional issues or trying to mask emotional pain never works.
- Self-harming behaviours bring short-lived results.
- Talk to someone about what is hurting. This pathway will lead to real change.

5.10. Controlling your anger

How people deal with their anger depends on their personality style. Some of us habitually lash out and become angry with the world, blaming everyone but ourselves. Some of us turn that anger inwards, blaming ourselves.

Anger is a normal emotion, though it clouds many other feelings that lie under it. Under anger there may also be humiliation, frustration, disappointment, and outrage. The most common emotion under anger is usually hurt. It is best to acknowledge and express why you are hurting, rather than get swept up in anger. For some people, it feels more acceptable to get angry and give back the anger rather than express hurt, or be tearful.

If you are a self-blamer who habitually turns anger in on yourself, it is time to stop making your life a misery. This is an entrenched pattern, and one you will need to keep tracking all your life. It is easy to be well balanced when things are calm. As soon as the stress levels rise, this is when you are likely to fall down a slippery slide into depressive thoughts, down old habitual neural pathways like, 'I have done it again, I am useless, I am hopeless, I should have seen that coming, I should have thought of that, I am an idiot, it is ALL my fault.'

At these times, take a big breath and ask yourself, 'What is the part I need to take responsibility for? What do I need to push back onto others instead of blaming myself?' You need to constantly remind yourself to take responsibility only for your part in the problem, and not blame yourself for everything. If you have this self-blaming kind of personality this is something that you will need to keep working on.

If you are an external blamer who lashes out verbally without thinking whenever you are hurting you will find that conflict surrounds you and stops you from getting your needs met. You might succeed on occasion by bullying someone into doing what you want, but you will find that people draw away from you and come to resent you. Hostility breeds hostility.

When you are feeling angry, allow yourself to feel the anger for a short time and quickly ask yourself the following questions: 'What am I really feeling? What is it I am really hurting about?' This is the hard part. If you search emotional vocabulary on the net, you will find there are many thousands of words to describe emotions. You can be annoyed, cross, disgusted, enraged, fed-up, exasperated, irritated, provoked, riled, seething, impatient, livid, disgruntled, and many more. Search for the words that reflect how you feel, because once you express them as the source of your anger, you will move to a calmer place.

There is also a good chance expressing your anger verbally will help other people understand you, too. Responding to situations with anger and hostility will only encourage more hostility to be directed back to you. No one likes to be spoken to in a hostile way, and a constant refuelling of anger serves no one. If you are feeling angry, ask yourself, 'Did this person mean to hurt me? What was the motivation behind what happened?' If you were someone else looking on, what would you see, and how would you view the situation?

If you are really overcome with anger and do not know why, it is important to take a step back until you do work out what it is that is hurting so much. Do not react. Count to 10. Breathe in deeply, and stop yourself from saying something that may inflame the situation. After all, you would have the capacity to stop yourself from swearing at a police officer, so you have the capacity to refrain in any other situation.

There is a deeper motivation for managing your anger. One day you may have your own family. Having children is the greatest test any human being can go through. It is tough dealing with children when they are sick, when you are sick, or both. How would you feel if you lost your temper to such an extent that you hurt your child? Go into training now so that you will be confident in your ability to hold expressions of anger and deal with the hurt in better ways than lashing out at others.

Violence is a learned behaviour. It is learned from people around you, and from media and video games. The more you are around violence, the more you may come to accept it as normal. If this is the case, stop! Step back and ask yourself how you are feeling about yourself. Is this the kind of person you wish to be? Physical or verbal abuse towards yourself or others is never an okay way of dealing with anger. Conflict is inevitable. Human beings will always disagree. You have to use better ways to resolve conflict.

It is your choice how you respond to stressful situations and how you choose to conduct yourself. Have the courage and insight to own whatever part you have in a conflict. Apologise for that, ask assertively for what you want, and refrain from lowering yourself to unacceptable aggressive behaviour.

Acknowledge conflict using good assertion skills. It is easy to play the, 'I'm not talking to you' game. This is being passive aggressive, and it's not healthy. Be upfront instead. Articulate what you think, feel, and prefer to happen, as this is more likely to get your needs met than engaging in a multitude of games. Remember, while broken bones mend in time, emotional scars can sometimes take even longer to heal. Be kind!

- Broken bones mend in time. Emotional scars take much longer.
- Be clear what you are hurting about.
- Learn to articulate what you need and what you prefer to happen.
- Take account of the motivation behind the hurt.
- Physical or verbal abuse toward yourself or others is NEVER okay.
- You choose how you respond and how you conduct yourself.

5.11. Resilience and leadership

Leadership opportunities will arise throughout your life. How you respond to them is a function of how confident you feel in managing your emotions, as well as your time. While it always feels easier to stay in our comfort zone, it is good to challenge yourself. Listen to your wants. If you really want to have a go at something, put your hand up and go for it. Trust yourself. You can do it!

If you would like to take on leadership roles, you have to start thinking of yourself as a leader. Instead of saying to yourself, 'I can't do that', switch your mind to saying, 'I can give that a go.' You have to hold in your head the image of you as a leader. Be brave; it is not as hard as you might think. Leadership roles can be fun, and they are great for your self-esteem.

If you are not quite ready for full leadership then challenge yourself to become a leader of you. Little by little, just step out of your comfort zone. Put yourself in training to become a leader of others by taking charge of yourself and your own thoughts. Give yourself challenges to overcome the things that scare you. If you are committed to your own personal growth, you will always be alert to challenges that will help you to learn something new. You will be open for opportunities to learn about your own capacities.

When you get the opportunity to lead others, there are some things to consider. Think about possibilities and outcomes, rather than jump too quickly with your ideas. Create a vision in your own head, and then share that with your team. Allow others to have their say. Use self-control – refrain from bulldozing them, as this is bullying and they will resent you for it. Show respect for other people's opinions; stress collaboration and cooperation. Remember, your team will respond to encouragement and the appreciation of work done well.

Ask your team to problem-solve. To do this, state the problem, present all relevant information and, together, list all the ideas so far. Evaluate each idea and come up with the most acceptable plan. It is important to always know everyone's name in your team, and to address them by their preferred name. Acknowledge your team's effort.

To truly lead, you need to motivate others by enthusing them about your ideas. If you listen carefully and incorporate other peoples' ideas into your plan then they will think it was their idea and will fully commit to it. Sometimes it might be useful to suggest some sort of challenge. Enter the challenge in fun, and provide rewards. Always appeal to the better side of other people and make it clear that you are honest and honourable. Show that you have integrity by having your actions match your word. This means you never two-faced, saying one thing out loud and another in private, or talking about a team member in a negative way to another. Monitor your own integrity and honesty.

As a leader, it's important to always be prepared, animated, and excited about your, and your team's ideas. Others love to be included in excitement, as well as having something to look forward to. When trying to persuade others, let them know what is in it for them – be open about the direction, and why they should take part. Empower your team members to grow and develop their own skills. Avoid micromanaging. Trust your team to come through with responsible behaviour.

- Hold a modest image in your head of yourself as a leader.
- Make the most of any leadership opportunity that comes your way.
- Build your self-esteem by stepping out of your comfort zone.
- Trust yourself. You can do it!
- Every leadership opportunity gives you a chance to learn new skills.

Chapter 6

6

Taking risks

6.1. Physical and emotional risks

6.2. Which is worse – taking, or not taking risks?

6.3. Finding your edge

6.4. Attracting good luck

6.5. Feeling real

6.6. Changing the scripts in your head

6.7. Good and bad decisions

6.8. Your future

6.1. Physical and emotional risks

Parents wish vehemently that they could make the world safe for their kids forever. It is amazing that toddlers don't get hurt more often as they explore their world. They plunge, often headfirst into obstacles, wobbling with their newfound ability to walk and having lots of crashes, yet their bones seem to be like rubber, and bruises heal rapidly. It seems that the older we get the more we are at risk of seriously injuring ourselves. Therefore, we need to assess physical risks more carefully. Failing to assess risks is just plain foolish.

Physical safety is one thing, emotional safety is another. Your choice of the company you keep is critical to your emotional wellbeing. It is easy to believe you can handle any emotional difficulty that comes your way. Remember that emotional scars can adversely affect your capacity to form sound relationships in the future. Your self-esteem is a precious part of you that needs to be cared for. If someone is demeaning you or disrespecting you on a regular basis, you need to put a halt to it. Always assess emotional risks. How will you protect your self-esteem if this continues?

One of your most important tasks in life is to take care of how you feel about yourself. Your emotional self is just as important as your physical self. Sometimes you will need to forgive yourself, as well as other people, because the territory of taking emotional risks comes with human error and mistakes.

Once you engage in a close relationship you put yourself at risk emotionally because you are not the only one in the equation. When others behave in ways that are immature, uncaring, or cruel, the resultant hurt can be devastating. The emotional repercussions of hurt can often be far worse than physical pain. The grief over the loss of a loved one or a lost relationship takes time to move through. If this happens to you, remember that it is not the end of the world. With sorrow often comes an appreciation of life, an appreciation of beauty, and a new beginning. Embrace this and move on.

- Your choice of the company you keep is critical to your emotional wellbeing.

6.2. Which is worse – taking, or not taking risks?

Living in fear of making mistakes is self-limiting. If you don't take risks then you are bypassing life. You may recall the saying, 'Nothing ventured, nothing gained.' It means that it is necessary to take risks to keep yourself healthy – to grow and learn. You will find out who you are by putting yourself out there and having a go at new things. It is important to remember to applaud yourself for the effort you put in, whether or not you have been successful.

It is easy to be too scared to try anything new. It is easy to fear what others might think. If you choose to go through life always playing it safe and never taking risks; you will miss out on so much. Try to make the risk-taking easy for yourself. You will be much more comfortable if you know you have analysed all the particular risks involved and have made a backup plan. If you have thought through all the possible outcomes and considered ways to protect yourself, then you can be free to enjoy the adventure, while still looking out for red flags.

With any kind of risk there is a possibility of stuffing up. It is easy to do this from time to time because we are human. Repeating the same mistakes over and over is what does ongoing damage to our self-esteem. Mistakes give us an opportunity to learn something new. It is not the mistake that counts, but rather what you learn from it that is important. Far better to make mistakes than to live in so much in fear that you miss out on all the future learning that comes with the territory.

The secret is to laugh at yourself before other people do. Humans make mistakes. Even in statistics and risk analysis it is described as human error. If you make a mistake, there is every chance that someone before you and someone after you will make the same, or similar mistake. Learn from it and move on!

If you are worried about what others think, look at it this way: it is very likely that those who are currently around you will not be part of your life in 10 years' time. What is important is that you're happy in yourself. If you make a mistake, you can say to yourself, 'Well, I stuffed that up – I'll never do that again!'

Risks without risk analysis is foolish behaviour. Take risks in a mindful way, knowing full well what you are risking, and why you want to take those risks. Know what you will gain or learn from the experience. When you do put yourself forward and take a risk, you will feel proud for having tried, regardless of the outcome.

- Nothing ventured, nothing gained!
- Living in fear of making mistakes is self-limiting.

6.3. Finding your edge

Taking calculated risks is what gives us a sense of adventure, excitement, and 'edge'. Edge is the space between what you hope for and the reality of your current life. It is the boundary where you meet your environment. It is the chasm you imagine between you and your dreams.

How you approach your edge gives a sense of who you are. Think about how you typically approach risk. Do you immediately shy away? Do you rush to defend your stance? Do you race in foolishly without thinking? Do you wholeheartedly just give it your best shot and have fun? How do you prepare and plan for success? Do you always think about worst-case scenarios? Are you happy with the way you approach edgy situations?

Think about how you want your life to be. Do you want to change it? Think about how you want to feel about yourself. Is your approach to risk healthy and productive? You can train yourself to hold back if you are inclined to rush in too quickly without thinking. You can spur yourself on if you know you tend to be too cautious. You can problem-solve and talk yourself through the backup plans so that you feel more comfortable taking a risk. You can help set situations up so you feel more confident.

Remember, if your brain goes too quickly down the, 'I'm too anxious to do anything like that' path, you can challenge yourself by asking yourself how much you want something. If you know how you approach risk, you can reassess and choose more productive ways. Your ability to challenge yourself, to push through anxious thoughts and take carefully calculated risks is what will change your life. Today you might challenge yourself to try a different food. Tomorrow you might talk to someone you have feared approaching. Think how much it will energise you and bring brightness into your life.

Everything in life involves risk. The only way to avoid risk is to stay at home and do nothing with your life. Even if you did this, you would be at risk of low self-esteem and poor mental health. Any sport or physical activity carries risk. It invigorates us and keeps life exciting. It is only when the costs outweigh the benefits that you will suffer.

As mentioned, taking an uncalculated risk is foolish. Jumping into a creek without considering the depth or likelihood of rock hazards is silly. No amount of bravado in the world will change that. Becoming physically injured through ill-considered actions would be extremely tragic.

Always have a backup plan when you take a risk. If you choose to go snowboarding on your own or in an isolated area, the experience may turn from exciting to tragic. To go out on the town with a group you don't know might be fun, but it could take you into dangerous situations. You always need a backup plan. Take your phone and always have money to get home. To be so inebriated or drugged that you are no longer in control of your actions, and are not in a safe environment with people who will look after you is not wise. It is likely to end with severe consequences.

Peer pressure and alcohol
A common trap is to get too caught up in the excitement of the moment. When others challenge you to compromise your own rules and principles, the peer pressure can place temptation

directly in front of you. After all, who wants to be thought of as a wuss in front of their friends? This kind of pressure is really tough to deal with. You know what is planned with your friends — think it through in advance, and have your response ready.

The classic mistake that young people tragically make is the quick decision to accept a ride from a friend who has had a few drinks. It is hard to know exactly what someone has drunk, and so easy to talk yourself into a situation that could end a life. Sometimes risks are just not worth taking. Be smart! Do not travel with anyone who has alcohol in their system. If you have been drinking yourself, know that once you have to ask yourself how many drinks you have had, you are in dangerous territory.

- Risk invigorates you and keeps life exciting.
- Taking a risk without a backup plan is foolish.
- Challenge yourself to push through anxious thoughts.
- Take carefully calculated risks, it will change your life.

6.4. Attracting good luck

Everyone seems to have their share of bad luck from time to time, though some seem to have bad luck more frequently than others. It is quite true that sometimes life happens in an extraordinary way, bringing a string of sheer bad luck. At those times you just have to shake your head and push through. Generally, the chances of bad luck can be minimised by responsibly taking as many precautions as is practical. This could mean arriving early enough to park in a well-lit area rather than having to walk down a dark alleyway, locking up properly, staying out of pubs after midnight, or not taking people who you have only just met to your flat or home. It might mean a simple thing like taking the trouble to buy a new battery for the torch you keep in the car for emergencies. You might complete your study tasks a little early in case you are sick or have something happen in the family that takes your time. It can be as simple as carrying your sneakers in your bag in case you get asked to try out for a team after school. It is checking that there is a spare tyre in good condition in the car, that brakes are attended to, and that windscreen wipers are working properly. It might mean setting the limit on what alcohol you will drink before you arrive at a party.

Being responsible means taking the trouble to organise things ahead of time so that life runs smoothly. Plan, organise, and take the initiative to minimise the chance of bad luck by maximising your chance of good luck. Be honest with yourself. Think intelligently about what you are doing, how efficient you are, and the repercussions of being slack. Self-check: are you really unlucky, or just a bit slack in preventing bad luck?

The other important element in good luck is having an attitude that is positive and hopeful. There is such a big game you can play with yourself along the lines of, 'If I always expect the worst then I won't have to deal with disappointment.' This is self-defeating; it is what I call a cop-out. The more you expect the worst-case scenario, the more likely you are to bring it on. You will get what you look for. If you search out negatives, that is exactly what you will find. Think of the possible consequences to all these things.

- Plan ahead.
- Take precautions to minimize the chance of bad luck.
- Avoid the 'if I think the worst I won't be disappointed' game. This is self-defeating.

6.5. Feeling real

When thinking about what gives you edge, one serious mistake is to think that this feeling of edge only comes from dangerous or illegal activities. I know graffiti artists who kid themselves that they are being edgy by creeping out at night and not getting caught, yet there is no way they would attempt abseiling. They confuse foolish danger with true grit.

I recall a young man who, at 17, was a talented artist staying out all night doing graffiti about town. He said he felt 'real', rather than just going along in a haze of boredom. He thrived on the adrenaline rush of not getting caught. At the same time he was too scared to show up to art classes and present his art. He had an underlying fear that if he really worked hard but didn't achieve high accolades or high marks then he would be exposed as not the fantastic artist he was made out to be.

Commonly, 16-17-year old boys will cease to try for fear of being seen as dumb or stupid. This is silly because it is based on the idea that it is so much better to gain notoriety as a rebellious student than risk being seen as a stupid one. The reality is that most people, deep down, doubt their own abilities and feel like a fraud in new situations. Anxious thoughts are normal when you are learning new things, are in a new job, or even when you are regarded as an expert. Mastery is something that comes with a lot of dedication, and that does not happen unless you have a sense of humility and appreciation of what you don't know. Self-doubt comes with this. You have a territory of new experiences. You have to get over feeling like a fraud and push those anxious thoughts aside. If self-doubt is so strong it paralyses you then you end up doing nothing. Such a waste!

Think about it. What if the young graffiti artist mentioned above had accepted that he had self-doubt? What if he had the humility to verbalise this to his teachers? What if he had put his full effort into his art? The risk would have paid off as he acquired a sense of success and purpose in his life with lots of reassurance from his teachers. Had he been brave and humble enough to just give it a go without fearing failure in front of his peers, he may well have gained the notoriety, accolades, and the marks that he craved. Instead he stopped trying and ran away while others plodded on. Unfortunately, this young man wasted years of his life until he finally realised that nothing would happen until he took the initiative to make it happen through accepting his self-doubt and simply having a go. If he had felt the edginess in his fear of failure, he could have thrived on it.

- It is normal to doubt your abilities when you do something new.
- Feeling like a fraud is normal until you are able to master your skill.
- Be honest with yourself about why you are avoiding real challenges.
- Trust yourself and applaud yourself for 'giving it a go.'
- Take calculated risks that help you feel proud of yourself and your achievements.

6.6. Changing the scripts in your head

What is a script?
A script is a set of phrases rehearsed repeatedly until they become automatic. Everyone acquires these in their head during childhood. These self-constructed stories bring perpetuating expectations and vary according to our experience. Sometimes they are positive, sometimes they are negative. Positive scripts include things like, 'I can do this,' 'I'll get another opportunity soon,' 'I can try,' and, 'I'll give it a go.'

The following are examples of negative scripts:

It's not fair.	No-one ever helps me.
I never get a chance.	I'm no good at that.
Nobody likes me.	I can't. I won't!
I can't compete.	I don't care!
I'm not good enough.	You've got it in for me.
I always lose.	I can't trust anyone.

While some scripts help you survive tough times, others can become troublesome when they linger on past their use-by date. As a child you may have acquired the script, 'I never get a chance'. As an adult this might be quite irrelevant when matched with reality, but the script keeps running and you draw back from new opportunities. The script is past its use-by date.

Scripts represents patterns of thinking that have developed strong neural networks. The brain will easily slip down them. When you have learned to ride a two-wheeler bike, the networks are strong; you just jump on the bike and ride it without thinking about all the steps of approaching or mounting the bike.

You learn these automatic scripts when you are young and dealing with tough or painful times. They become outdated, but still influence your present existence. If you are not careful, these scripts can run in the background for your entire life unless you confront and challenge them. Rather than be programmed by your past choices, renew yourself with new scripts.

To take control of your most frequent or troublesome scripts, you need first to identify what they are, and then examine them for their usefulness. Test their reality, and if they are destructive to your current life then they need to be pushed aside. Negative scripts need to be replaced with something that reflects a positive attitude to growth. Develop a positive perspective, for example: 'I need to start trusting people more,' or, 'I need to start having a go.' Be aware of your usual scripts. Once you are aware, you are already on the pathway to being able to change.

Spinning stories – who is fooling who?
While some people seem to be naturally open and honest, others feel the need to spin stories in order to not lose face, or to disguise feelings of inadequacy. This is unfortunate because life throws up many challenging situations, and there is no shame in feeling inadequate. Habitually running stories in your head can entice you into believing the stories are real and true. Dishonest stories do considerable damage to relationships. Regardless of the size of the story, relationships are spoiled when someone uses dishonesty to manipulate another.

If you tell a story that you don't like water skiing because you think it is a dumb sport, others might suspect that the real truth is that you are not confident in the water. To challenge you on this would seem mean because it would be drawing attention to something you feel is a weakness. Listeners are more likely to back away rather than say anything that will offend you. They are more likely to carry on the façade. This means that neither person is interacting in an honest way. The relationship becomes fake.

I have noticed that otherwise highly-intelligent people sometimes think that no one else can see through the little twists and half-truths they spin. Following initial success, they develop more and more complex emotional games to reinforce their position. Ultimately, they come to fool themselves into believing these manipulations. Whether conscious or unconscious, they think they are so smart and so skilful in their story weaving that no one else will ever catch on. Insincerity, glossing over, power plays, or emotional blackmail are characteristic strategies used. These games are all designed to manipulate others for one's own benefit.

Emotional blackmail

It is one thing to misrepresent the truth to embellish or escalate a story. It is another thing to deliberately include a piece of information in order to get attention or sympathy. It might be something like, 'Poor me, no one likes me, I am unlovable,' or, 'I don't have any true friends.' If you make comments intended to get someone else to take pity on you, to affirm or praise you, or benefit you in some way then you are being emotionally manipulative. Conditional love is not love.

If you question another person's love, or suggest they don't love you because they won't do what you want them to do, then you are engaging in emotional blackmail. The end result may be that you get your way, but you will lose out in the big picture. Ultimately, you will create emotional distance between you and the person you are hurting. They might still love you, but you will lose the respect that is needed to sustain a healthy relationship.

You have to understand that targets of emotional blackmail find themselves in a no-win situation. If they meet the manipulator's wishes they become embroiled in a false relationship. If they reject the wishes, they buy into the manipulator's story of being unloved, and therefore become complicit in a flawed relationship. Emotional manipulators fool themselves into believing they have won, whereas the target of the emotional blackmail withdraws and moves away emotionally.

Reflecting on this, it is easier to be open and honest than to sustain consistent story-making. You can fool yourself that others are believing your stories, but sooner or later people will wake up. They will move away from you emotionally. They will retreat, and have no investment in being your friend. Even family members can't help you. If this is you, then it is something you need to change yourself. Accept yourself as a fallible human being who is not ever going to be perfect at everything. If you are open and honest about your failings you will be lovable.

Remember, it is so easy to get sucked into a story of your own making. It is your choice. You can choose to be seen as a dishonest person who manipulates others to get what you want, or you can choose to be seen as a person who has integrity. The most important person you need to be honest with is yourself.

- While some scripts help us survive tough times, the same scripts can become troublesome when they linger on past their use-by date.
- Tiny stories that emotionally manipulate others are easily seen through.
- It is easier to be open and honest than sustain consistent story-making.
- No matter how clever you are, others will always see through emotional blackmail.

6.7. Good and bad decisions

Knowing what you want is tricky. You have been told since you were little not to think about what you want because that is selfish, yet, knowing what you want is critical to setting goals. It is quite normal to be indecisive. There are lots of decisions you are called on to make as you get older. Adults often feel indecisive about changes in their life. This is quite normal. The trouble is, worrying about making a wrong decision will often lead you to avoid making one at all. When this happens, life tends to make decisions for us. This may be through default, or by someone stepping in to choose. These people can include your parents, teachers, and principals and, if this happens, it means that you will have to leave missed opportunities behind.

The thing is, as with most big decisions, you can never know whether it will be the right one or not. Once the decision is made, the pathway is set and you can't go back in time. It is like being at a fork in the road. You take one path and never know where the other one leads to unless you choose to go down it at a later time. Sometimes you just have to go with a decision, and find where the journey takes you. You will never know the end result of where the other pathway may have led.

It is important to remember that if you don't like the journey you have chosen you can always make another decision down the track that will divert you towards a different path. Sometimes a dead end will teach you more about what you want in life. Doing this is as simple as tuning into your heart and your passions, and having the confidence to choose the pathway that will build your self-esteem. We each have our own unique set of interests and talents that we need to foster. Build your capacity to know what you want so that your potential can be harnessed.

This is not easy. Practise choosing at every point of the day. Start small – do you want toast with honey or Vegemite? Do you want to go outside and shoot hoops, or read a book? Make these choices mindfully, and practice your wanting. The more choices you make, the better you come to know yourself and what you want. Your capacity to choose is like a muscle that needs flexing all the time. Build your choice muscle with increasingly important decision-making. Mindful choice defines who you are, what you want, and what you don't want. It takes practice.

- Worrying too much about making a wrong decision will likely lead you to avoid making one at all.
- Sometimes in life you have to take a leap of faith, to follow your heart and just 'go with it'.
- If you dislike the chosen pathway you can change direction.
- Mindful choice helps define who you are, what you want and what you don't want.

6.8. Your future

Worrying about the future is an issue that seems to run in the background for most young people. Rather than worry, it is better to be constructive and work out all the elements that will help you decide on your career or employment pathway.

Firstly, bring into awareness all the things that you are interested in. Do you have a passion or a strong interest in any area? Secondly, think about your strengths. Are you good at talking to people? Are you a quick thinker, or a steady worker? Do you like to focus on one thing at a time, or to be very busy with lots of things happening at once? Do you like to be moving around, or working in one place? Find someone who knows you well and ask them what they think your special strengths are. This can help you to stand back and view yourself with all your potential.

Thirdly, set about collecting as much information as possible. If you have an interest in working with animals, then research every job you can find that deals with animals. Look to see what jobs are advertised, what training courses are at TAFE or university, and talk to the local vet. Ask them what they like most about the job, and what is the hardest part. Are there other places where vets work? Put thought into the questions you would like answered. Be creative about who you might be able to ask about the career you have an interest in. Treat this like a very important project. Keep a journal of what you find out, and write information down. When things are written down the information feels more manageable than when it is floating around unstructured in your head.

Finally, when you have thought about a few careers that hold interest for you, have a discussion with your parents, carers, or family friends. Quiz them about all the different kinds of industries that are around so that you can identify a few that you have interest in.

This is not an exercise to find the very career you will have for the rest of your life. This is purely an awareness stage to learn what is out there. It would be wonderful if you came up with 20-30 careers that hold interest, as well as a few industries. For each career on your list, set about to identify the prerequisites you need for various entry points into the career and the industry. The more information you gain, the easier you will feel about your subject choices and decision-making. You will go through a process of elimination and gradually arrive at the pathway that feels right for you.

You may find that you have two or three career pathways that you can explore. Remember, it is quite common for various interests to come together down the track, often giving you a very unique career. For instance, someone might be interested in being a tour guide and also work in graphic design. One day they might find work in advertising as a promoter of adventure leisure activities. Who knows where all your interests might lead? Keep actively engaged in all that interests you.

If you have learned to get along well with others in team efforts, can be flexible in your attitude to learning new things, have the opportunity to develop your initiative, are able to analyse and problem-solve difficulties, and quickly learn new things, then you will be a sought-after employee. There are some attributes that you could work on: good manners, respect for others, patience, common sense, integrity, having a strong moral code of behaviour, being trustworthy, being kind and caring, having a sense of fun, and being keen to learn. These sort of attributes will bring you many rewards in the future, and are ones that you can cultivate in yourself.

Every experience in the workforce will provide you with skills and new learning, so don't worry if you meet dead ends. Sometimes knowing what you do not want to do is a powerful way to finding out what it is you do want.

Rather than worry about the future, just focus on where you are right now and identify what feels comfortable and exciting. If you have a notion that you would like to work as a mechanic, then go with it. Get adult support to seek out a mechanic to talk to, and maybe even ask for work experience. You may find you love it, or you may decide that it has absolutely no interest for you. Either way you will be further on your decision journey.

Make sure you do not limit your dreams by thinking, *I could never do that*. Remember that when you go to a training institution it is their role to teach you what you need to know in order to carry out duties in the chosen field. As long as you have the passion and the willingness to do what they ask of you, you will find that you gradually acquire all the skills and knowledge you will need. Trust the training process and follow your dreams.

- Explore and identify your strengths and the activities you enjoy.
- Search out detailed information about industries and entry points.
- It is the job of the training institutions to teach you what you need to know to be competent.

Chapter 7

7

Nurturing your soul

7.1. Believing in yourself

7.2. Spirituality and you

7.3. Going forward

7.1. Believing in yourself

The world is a crazy place, full of both wonderful and awful things. It is great to have a sense of justice, but at some stage we have to accept that life is not fair. You can't win every argument, or force others over to the way you think. You can only influence people by giving them another perspective if they are open to a receiving it. Believe in yourself, even when others try to talk you down.

When you feel frustrated and blocked because others are stuck in what you know to be ill-founded beliefs or ignorance, the best you can do is to search for the deeper point from which they diverge from yours – the bit where they do agree with you. If they aren't going to hear you at all, save your energy and actions. Instead, look for convincing ways to be heard in more strategic circles. When you find your passion, go for it. Don't listen to negative or pessimistic people. Don't be dispirited by them in the short-term. Aim for the future!

Know that while you might have many endearing characteristics, you are no different from other people when it comes to daily life, needs, and body functions. We are all ordinary human beings, though each of us has different hopes, dreams, passions, and strengths. That is what makes us unique. Everyone has fearful thoughts running through their heads. Everyone has self-doubt, and disappointments. What makes the difference is that some choose to dwell on those, while others push them aside and forge ahead.

If you put other people above you, you will feel less than. You don't need to do that. Be inspired by someone else's efforts, but don't diminish yourself. Listen to others, but value your own thoughts. Rather than worrying about what others think, celebrate your own efforts and how you feel about yourself for having given full effort.

Learn to go with the flow. Rather than stressing over exams or study tasks, put 100% focus into them. Work hard, over-prepare, then chill out. Enjoy each day. Remember, this day you will never have again. Do something each day that brings happiness to your soul. At the same time, be sensible in the way you protect yourself from scary situations. Avoid walking in dark places alone at night. Just don't do it! Think about who you choose to spend your time with, and never be alone with someone you don't know.

Nurturing your soul is also about protecting your physical and emotional self so as to avoid trauma. When you do walk alone, walk in a businesslike way that indicates you have to be somewhere. Rather than saunter, walk confidently with your head held high, and be aware of those around you.

Try to build a life where your circumstances nurture your soul. Some think of a soul as being the totality of ourselves; a combination of every aspect of 'you', such as thoughts, feelings, beliefs, and an awareness of our internal and external worlds. Whatever a soul is to you, know that when your head, heart, and body are all focused in the here and now, you are in a good spiritual space and your soul is being nurtured. If you forget to nurture your soul by not experiencing the joy of being in the moment in your daily world, you will end up feeling disconnected and out of sorts. You may even start listening more to your anxious thoughts.

Look to your internal awareness, to your hopes, dreams, and yearnings. This is an important part of self-care. Practice the art of being in the moment – a pleasant state of being comfortable with your thoughts and emotions, both separate and together.

- Believe in yourself, even when others try to talk you down.
- Instead of worrying what others think, trust in your decision-making.
- Celebrate your success.

7.2. Spirituality and you

The ability to be in the here and now is a critical part of many spiritual practices. If you can achieve mindfulness for a good part of the day you will feel a sense of wellbeing. The sense of your own spirituality comes when you are fully engaged in something important to you, something you enjoy. For some, it may be through sport, music, prayer, learning, or experiencing the environment. Remember, spirituality is not something that is owned by, or only available to you, through religion. Find your own spiritual way of being in the world.

Be very wary of cults and groups that have a stifling religious or mystical belief system outside the mainstream religions. If you join any type of group or following that engulfs your time, or tries to control you in any way, regard this as a red flag. There are skillful persuaders who use narrowing processes to confine your experience of the outside world in order to bombard and seduce; to brainwash you into becoming a passionate believer. These organisations seek financial gain and power but their motivation might not be apparent at first.

When life feels confusing, it is very tempting to accept black and white explanations of life because the mystical elements linked to the talk are enticing. To believe in mystical powers greater than yourself disempowers you in holding and shaping your own life. Promises of enlightenment and being lifted to a higher stage of awareness are often accompanied by cunning motivators. It is true that if you believe enough you can brainwash yourself into believing this greater being has changed your life.

Believe in yourself and your power to choose your own destiny, rather than have it allotted to you or controlled by a suspect higher being. It is so easy to rush into subscribing to black and white views of the world that bring a sense of security because they seem to have all the answers. It is much harder to live with the ambiguity of the unknown, but at least it stops you from being sucked into simplistic and erroneous thinking.

There are enough wondrous and mystical things in *real* life if you seek them. Think about what you want to change in your life, work towards that, and reap the benefits of satisfaction and joy in the lifestyle you have achieved for yourself. Enjoy the simple pleasures. If mundane jobs take you down that path, then don't think they are beneath you. Rather than search for happiness, or see it as a right, use your wisdom to know that it will come as a byproduct of dedication and commitment. Following your passions will bring you to that magical sense of wonder and beauty. You have it within you!

- Find your special activity that helps to keep you in the moment.
- Be wary of skillful persuaders who try to simplify your faith and your life.
- Coach yourself to live with ambiguity. The world is a confusing place.
- Rather than search for happiness, follow your passions and happiness will be a by-product.

Wisdom

When you are caught up in the world of others, you miss the little things; the sparks of brilliance, and the joys of nature. If you take time to be in the present, to be more attentive in your observation of reality, you will regenerate your spirit and gain insight into your needs and wants. Wisdom brings you to appreciate your own spirituality in relation to others; it demands living with an unconditional openness to hold one or more views at once. Wisdom means living with an understanding that life has many shades of grey, and that nothing about life is simple.

Wisdom means having the ability to tolerate ambiguity and complexity, rather than holding on to rigid and simplistic views of the world because it is easier and less distressing. Rigid and closed thinking inevitably leads to judgement and prejudice. With wisdom you can learn to live with, rather than to fear complexity. Once you learn to do this you are also able to appreciate the simplicity of life in the here and now.

Wisdom brings a sense of balance in changing contexts. No matter the situation, wisdom tells you that you will be okay. It means not changing ourselves to suit the environment or social scene, but rather being ourselves in every context. Be yourself, not who you think others want you to be!

> - Wisdom brings a sense of balance in changing contexts.

Humility

Humility is different to wisdom, but is equally important. It is the idea of not having to win at all costs; not feeling better than, and not finding fault with everyone else. Humility is not always having to be right; it is realising that there is always something you can learn from another. To achieve humility, listen before you speak and allow others to talk instead of you dominating conversation.

Make room for others without losing the ability to stand up for something when it counts. Remember that people with big egos often have little or no capacity to hear or learn from others. Humility recognises that your greatest gifts and strengths in one context often prove to be your greatest weakness in other areas. Being a dominant and confident speaker in a debate may not equip us in intimate conversation. Similarly, being a kind and caring person who puts others first may not be helpful in having one's own needs met.

Humility brings the ability to adapt as you grow towards and through dreams that challenge you. It is understanding that you have much to learn. You can habitually give up too easily when you fail unless you have enough humility to own your failure, to try again and grow past it. You can play games like, 'Poor me,' or you can act in a belligerent way by refusing to grow and learn. This will work; it will get you out of things. Others will eventually back away and leave you alone. The end result is that you will likely feel lonely, have low self-esteem, lack personal dignity, and your life experience will be narrow.

It is so easy to stop ourselves from growing; to block ourselves from making the best of our life by taking too much notice of fear; fear of losing face, of being embarrassed, of the unknown, of competition, of being shamed, that you will never change, or that you won't be able to handle emotional intimacy. Fear can block you at every step unless you learn to push anxious thoughts out of your focus. A positive attitude to learning and growth tells you that it is worth trying new things because you will always learn something. The more you learn, the more you will grow as a person.

To do this, you need to draw on your strong emotional self to plough your way through every anxious thought that gets in the way of your dreams. Rather than hold yourself back, follow your heart and your dreams. Push the fear aside. If you add a little wisdom and humility you will have the perfect recipe to come to appreciate who you really are.

Your attitude to new experiences is what will shape your life. A positive attitude affects the way you learn, and the way you take on challenges. Interest leads to connections with others and with new ideas. Out of dreadful situations can come good experiences if you have the humility to connect with others, and a positive attitude towards finding new pathways.

Your attitude to success will reveal your arrogance or your humility. It is so important to take a little time out to feel good about what you have achieved. Arrogant people will gloat and broadcast how great they are. They will rub it in to those who have been defeated. Humble people will celebrate their success and allow themselves to be exuberant amongst family and friends, but they won't highlight the weakness of others, or make them feel bad or sad in any way. They won't brag or exaggerate their brilliance, but rather be meek about it, acknowledging the fine competition or hard work exhibited by their competitors. It is in your hands. You can choose to be arrogant, or humble and gracious about the defeat of other.

A positive attitude will propel you forward; a negative attitude will make you static and unchanging. With polite words and patience, a little enthusiasm will go a long way. Rarely will you see things in reality because you look through the lens of your own experience, but think about what you do every day to invest in a positive attitude. You will find that when you take the time and trouble to look at things positively, everything around you will change. You can choose what you want and how you want to be.

- Humility means listening before you speak.
- Be yourself rather than who you think others want you to be.
- Humility is not having to always be right or being quick to fault others.
- A positive attitude will attract others to join you.

7.3. Going forward

When you change who you are, it is like saying goodbye to an old friend. It feels uncomfortable for a while, but eventually the New You will look back at the Old You as a distant thing of the past. Every day brings change of one kind or another. Follow your dreams but be sure to ground them in gratitude for all the positive aspects of your life. Take time out to think about your dreams, but dreams themselves can be hollow. It is the journey that has to be enjoyed. Start with some dreams, and be prepared to modify them as you change your direction in response to things that grab you passionately along the journey.

Just as you connect in to social media, take time to connect in with yourself once in a while. If you are too busy, you might find that your thoughts are all over the place, and the mundane things seem more important than the essentials. If you are too busy, everything seems overly important and you become more in tune with what is happening in everyone else's lives instead of your own. You might find you are irritable or resentful of the demands others put on you. If you see these signs, take time out. Make doing nothing a high priority for a while as you gather your strength and your focus on what is important.

Love unconditionally, but not foolishly. Cherish your good friendships, and be on the lookout for others who are judgemental, or don't share your values of kindness to others. If relationships fall apart, think about what you have learned about yourself and others, and don't be afraid to say goodbye to those who want to hurt you for their own purposes. Trust that you will find someone who will love you for who you are, not who they want you to be. Respect and cherish your family – they will walk beside you your whole life. Remember, the smallest gift is a treasure and may be all that another can give.

You can become whoever you want to be! You can build your personality and your character. Value your strengths, build on them, and enthusiastically pursue your pathway with whatever passion you have. Try to be honest with yourself and make your actions match your words. As you live your life with integrity, this will set you apart from others and make you outstanding!

Remember, life has its ups and downs – without one, there is no appreciation of the other. Without sadness, there is no appreciation of joy, so enjoy the rollercoaster, knowing you won't be down for very long; there is always an exhilarating hill ahead. Enjoy the success that comes with calculated risk. Focus, work hard and enjoy a journey full of fun. Your rewards will be many!

Harness your thoughts, emotions and body in determining how you want to live your life. When you do this you will find yourself to be much more than the sum of all your parts.

- Have gratitude for all the positive aspects of your life.
- Change is uncomfortable and is an integral part of living.
- Life has its ups and downs.
- Value your own unique strengths and build on them.
- Make choices that will enhance your self-esteem and build your resilience.
- Try to love unconditionally, but not foolishly.
- Respect and cherish your family, they are your greatest allies.

Work out what you want and choose how you want to be!

About the author

Following an early career as a commerce teacher, Helen gained a Master's degree in Education Studies in 1993, and worked as a Guidance Officer in Queensland schools for 15 years. During this time she continued her studies with a two year post-graduate training program in family therapy. She became a Registered Psychologist and completed a second Master's degree in 2006 in Gestalt Therapy.

The same year, Helen moved to Hobart and worked in EAPs (Employee Assistance Programs) and in private practice. Missing work with young people, she took on regular days at Headspace in 2009, working with 12-26 year olds. She delights in working with adolescents who are often unguarded in the way they speak their mind, and open their hearts.

Helen gained generalist experience across a wide variety of contexts. In secondary schools she was involved in program development for tertiary entrance, pathways planning, student welfare, special needs, critical incident planning, and behaviour management. As a school counsellor she worked with students, parents, and staff. She also assisted students with career and academic counselling. Her employee assistance work involved trauma assist, manager assist and employee assist services. In private practice she continues to work with adolescents, young adults, couples, and families.

She looks back on her career having been honoured by the trust that young people, in particular, have placed in her. In her book she has highlighted the complexity of issues that confront young adults. She hopes the book propels them into wise choice-making throughout their lives.

Helen currently lives in beautiful Hobart, Tasmania. She is semi-retired, enjoys time with her grandchildren, travelling with her husband, keeping fit, and staying in touch with friends.